# Testimonials

"*Joan's Greatest Administrative Secrets Revealed* sets the gold star standard of what it critically takes to be a stellar Executive Assistant. This is no ordinary, run of the mill how-to book. Joan's tell-it-like-it-is style is raw, powerful and poignant. Her 'white gloves off' approach finally fills in the mysterious gaps of what it really takes to not only develop ourselves personally to shatter our own glass ceilings, but to obtain and sustain that elusive brass ring of a true strategic partnership with our Executives that even the most seasoned Executive Assistant is searching for, but that all levels of Assistants must truly know, live and practice to succeed and thrive."

**WENDE MORROW**
Senior Executive Assistant to the CEO, R&R Partners
32 Years in the Administrative Profession

——

"Having had the privilege of working with Joan Burge for more than ten years, I can attest to the fact that reading this book is just like sitting down with Joan over coffee and receiving her valuable wisdom of the administrative profession. This book is for the adventurous assistant looking to elevate their career. Joan is bold, she's a visionary, she expects us to get out of our comfort zone and SHINE. If you're willing to embrace what Joan shares and believe in yourself as you put her tips to the test, you're in for an epic ride!"

**JASMINE FREEMAN**
Assistant to the Chief of Public Safety, City of Las Vegas
20 Years in the Administrative Profession

——

"This is the playbook we needed! A must have for all administrative professionals! I love how Joan includes more stories from her own career, as well as thought-provoking questions throughout the entire book. Each chapter will definitely challenge you to think out of the box as you focus to elevate your performance and continue on your career journey. So, grab your flags and highlighters, you are going to need them!"

**SHERRY VIERING**
Senior Executive Administrative Assistant
25 Years in the Administrative Profession

——

"*Joan's Greatest Administrative Secrets Revealed* is just that! Joan Burge, CEO/Founder of Office Dynamics International, Speaker, Trainer, Consultant, and former Executive Assistant has combined her expansive business experience with her true passion for administrative excellence to create this no-nonsense book. Joan provides her Greatest Administrative Secrets or best techniques to address day-to-day issues encountered in the office. Each chapter is relevant, enlightening, and will challenge your thinking all while inspiring you to succeed. No matter if you are an entry level or seasoned professional - if you are serious about your career, this how-to book is a must read."

**LAURA SUCHOCKI, CWCA, CEAP**
Lead Executive Assistant
40 Years in the Administrative Profession

——

"If you really are going to invest in yourself and your career, USE THIS BOOK! Make it part of your personal improvement plan and revisit it monthly to make sure you are staying on track or tweak your plan if need be. I stayed riveted to each page and read some sections twice just to be sure that I was capturing what Joan was sharing. This book promises the revelation of secrets from Joan learned across a lifetime of hard work, tenacity, and an interminable quest for professional excellence. Mission accomplished!"

**MICHELLE B. PENNINGTON**
Office Administrative Assistant
30 Years in the Administrative Profession

——

"I have had the pleasure of knowing Joan Burge for nearly 20 years. Joan demonstrates the necessity of human interaction and how taking the time to make a phone call or have a face-to-face meeting can prevent misunderstandings, strengthen relationships, and build a network. If you take away just one thing from reading this book, trust that Joan cares enough to tell us the honest truth, (even when it's difficult to hear), and it is our successes that Joan loves to celebrate with us."

**SUE M. VELARDE**
Human Resources Support
36 Years in the Administrative Profession

——

"This book will become the standard go to manual for every administrative professional at every experience level. Joan shares her decades of experience not only as an executive assistant but as a mentor, an executive, a presenter, and a business owner. The straight forward advice Joan shares is written with boldness because she wants each reader to realize their potential. Joan shares all of the essential best practices for both personal and professional fulfillment. These methods are proven successful by Joan's own examples and experience. There are numerous ways to personalize this book for your own unique journey. This book will become your personal manifesto."

**DANA BUCHANAN (.COM)**
Senior Administrative Assistant and Writer
20+ Years in the Administrative Profession

——

"This is one of the most impactful books I have ever read. Joan has a no-nonsense and matter-of fact-approach to encouraging others to always continue learning, take risks, and step outside of your comfort zone. Her advice and stories on how she handled various challenges and bosses left me wondering if I handled specific situations in my administrative career with the same grace and wisdom."

**JONI HOGUE**
Executive Assistant
33 Years in the Administrative Profession

——

# JOAN'S
## GREATEST ADMINISTRATIVE
## SECRETS REVEALED

**By Joan M. Burge**

Published by Office Dynamics International
Las Vegas, Nevada

Book Cover Design by Brian Burge (Las Vegas)
Photography by Chris Tucker (Las Vegas)

For information and inquiries:
Office Dynamics, 5575 S. Durango Dr., Suite 106,
Las Vegas, NV 89113 or call 1-800-782-7139

ISBN: 978-1-7321221-0-9

# Books by Joan Burge

*Assistants and Executives Working in Partnership:*
*The Definitive Guide to Success*

*Who Took My Pen . . . Again?*

*Give Yourself Permission to Live a BIG Life*

*Underneath It All: Postgraduate Level Revelations Lift*
*Administrative Assistants to New Heights*

*Become an Inner Circle Assistant*

*Real World Communication Strategies That Work*

*The Survival Guide for Novice Entrepreneurs*

*The Survival Guide for Secretaries and Administrative Assistants*

# Joan Burge
# Administrative Visionary, Industry Pioneer, and Catalyst for Change

Joan Burge is known as the pioneer of the administrative training industry. Joan is an accomplished author, professional speaker, consultant and corporate trainer.

In 1990, Joan created a business in an untapped niche, overcoming monumental obstacles involving corporations' and managers' attitudes, prejudices and stereotypes about executive assistants and administrative professionals. Joan dedicated herself to inspiring excellence and encouraging administrative professionals to reach for the stars! Her company, Office Dynamics International, is a global industry leader that offers a broad range of solutions and provides high-performance, sophisticated executive and administrative assistant training and coaching.

One thing is clear: Executive assistants, their executives, HR business partners, administrators, and managers have come to rely on Office Dynamics International because "only Joan is Joan." Joan Burge is an original, the foremost expert in the demanding field of management support. She put in the hard work and extensive investment required to earn the reputation of excellence and uncompromising trust of leaders in business. Through her empowering teaching, Joan illuminates building better work relationships between executives and their assistants.

Joan's never-ending quest to provide top-notch educational programs has earned the respect of premier clients like Walt Disney World, Procter & Gamble, Cisco Systems, Battelle, AT&T, Boeing, Humana Inc., Sunoco, Nokia, and Nationwide Insurance.

She is best known for her highly-acclaimed Star Achievement Series® course, which promotes 'Star Performance' among executive assistants and administrative staff. This flagship training program has inspired thousands of administrative professionals to achieve excellence.

Joan is the creator and host of the Annual Conference for Administrative Excellence™ (started in 1993); the World Class Assistant™ professional designation course; and more than 250 customized workshops for executive and administrative assistants. Joan has produced more than 350 educational videos and written more than 500 articles.

Joan has authored four groundbreaking books for administrative professionals including the Amazon Best Seller *Who Took My Pen … Again?* Her administrative career "bibles" entitled *Become an Inner Circle Assistant* and *Underneath It All* continue to be favorites among executives and administrative assistants worldwide.

*CAUTION: This book is pure Joan Burge: unabridged, and unapologetic.*

## Dear Adventurer,

If you are looking for a book that will teach you how to plan meetings, book travel, schedule appointments, or work with Microsoft Office, this is not it. This book is filled with the behaviors, actions, thoughts, and strategies that will change your world.

Whether you choose to stay in the administrative profession or move into another profession, these proven principles will lead you to unprecedented success. These secrets are powerful and it is the combination of using all these secrets that will explode like a bonfire.

How do I know? Because I lived every one of these ideas when I worked in the administrative profession for 20 years, and I have been teaching these ideas to assistants since 1990 when I started my training company, Office Dynamics International. Having worked in the administrative profession for so many years, I know your challenges, frustrations, and fears. I speak your language. I also know that you have tremendous potential and can grow and excel if you will learn my secrets for success and apply them to your life.

Prior to this book, I have written four books for assistants. Typical of many authors, I always hired someone to soften the edges of my writing or maybe say something a little more eloquently. The reason is because many times when I write a book, article, or blog, I am focused on what I want the reader to know rather than how I am saying it.

When I conceived this book idea, I decided I wanted this book to be 'pure' Joan Burge. I wanted to write this book with freedom and in a manner that is truly me. If you and I were sitting in a coffee shop chatting about your career and you asked for my advice, I would tell you what I have written in this book, in these words. I may not say it exactly the way you would like to receive the information, but this is how I have helped tens of thousands of assistants improve the quality of their personal and professional lives.

Throughout the book, you will see a lot of bullet point tips. That is because I tend to communicate straight forward, direct, and to the point. I also recognize that today people don't have a lot of time to sift through tons of information to get to the meat. Your time is valuable.

My main intent is to challenge your thinking, to push you beyond the status quo, because I know you are capable of much more than what you are doing today. You have just scratched the surface of what I know you can do. We grow when we feel uncomfortable because we have to navigate differently, think contrarily, seek solutions, be creative, learn to adapt, and reach out to others for help. That is when the real magic happens!

Before you begin reading this book, I highly recommend you gather a pen, highlighters, and Post-it® notes. You will want to highlight ideas that really stand out for you or have special meaning. Write notes in the margins. Stick little or big Post-its® on pages you want to revisit. See this book as your 'work book.' Keep it on your desk and refer to it often. Share great ideas with your peers and your leader.

I truly care about each and every assistant and that includes you! So, after you have read the book, I would love to hear your thoughts. Please feel free to write me at burgej@officedynamics.com.

Best of luck going on this journey! I hope to meet you in person some day at one of our live events.

—JOAN BURGE

# Table of Contents

# CHAPTER
# 1

# THE BIG SECRET!

**I AM OFTEN ASKED** what is the secret to being an outstanding assistant? There is no one big secret that will make you a star assistant; there is no single thing that you can do to be a star. To be a star assistant you have to do **101** things well! That includes everything from handling phone calls to managing emails, planning travel, arranging meetings, keeping your leader organized and on time, making decisions, being solution-driven, taking the initiative, employing excellent communication skills to direct issues to the 'right' person and keeping your executive updated on what's going on in the office.

I understand this is a tall order and can be intimidating. Remember, I was an executive assistant for twenty years and I worked in twelve different companies in five states. It was not unusual for executives to expect me to deliver my best work. That does not mean I did deliver the very best every day, year after year. I certainly committed to doing my best and giving my best. But life happens and it happened to me and my family during those twenty years.

One thing, though, is that when I knew I wasn't performing at my optimum I talked to my executive about it. I didn't want my executive to think I didn't care about my job or my work. I assured my executive that I would get back on track. Do you know what? My executive was always understanding and supportive.

So how do you—how did I—do 101 things well? Here are a few ideas to get you started.

- Master your craft. Don't ever assume you know everything and you do it to the best of your ability because you will never seek new ways and new answers. You will get into a rut and eventually become obsolete.

- Pay attention to the details. This is a vital component of your role. As they say, "The devil is in the details." That has been proven to me many times over the years, even as a CEO and business owner.

- Write things down. Do not assume you are going to remember every little thing you have to do or your executive tells you. Whether you are getting information from a caller or visitor or coworker, make notes. It's very hard in this age of distraction and interruption to remember everything. If you are a star assistant, you will capture information like crazy!

- Listen. This is probably one of the strongest skills you can employ. When you listen, you catch the details. When you listen, you get a fuller picture of what is going on. Listening reduces errors, rework, and frustration. When we fully listen—and I mean fully—we are absorbed in the moment. We listen with our brains.

- Ask other assistants about their best practices. I loved working with other assistants who knew more in certain areas than I did because they made my life easier. When I worked at Coppertone in Memphis, Tennessee, there were two great assistants who sat on either side of my cubby. Yes, it was noisy and drove me crazy sometimes, but there were more benefits than negatives to having my peers close to me. Each of the two assistants was smart in different areas. Plus, both had been working at Coppertone for a while so they showed me the ropes.

- Study. There is no way around it. If you are going to shine in 101 areas in this profession, you need to keep up with what is going on in the profession. Thank goodness times are much different today for assistants than 30 and 40 years ago. The information available to you for your chosen profession is astounding. My company alone offers more than 100 courses for assistants, has published more than 1500 blogs, produced 250 educational videos, 300+ articles (as of this writing), hosts webinars and conferences, and this is my fifth book for assistants!

- Read everything that crosses your path. It really doesn't take that long. I realize it is difficult because we have volumes of information available to us. You do need to be selective. The idea is that when you read about a variety of things, you become more confident. You are in the know. I have always been an avid reader of interesting subjects and especially anything related to the business world. Nowadays, I read in little chunks because I simply am too busy. That might be a good practice for you. Just take a few minutes here and there throughout the day at work and at home to read.

- Practice, practice, practice. How do you think athletes make it to the Olympics? How does someone win on "Dancing with the Stars"? Why are certain football or basketball players in such high demand? Because they are really good at what they do. The only way for you to get great at the skills you need to be a star assistant is to practice over and over. Before you know it, that 'thing' will become a part of you. It's like when I started professional speaking and training. I didn't know what I was doing. I was scared to death. I just kept speaking in front of groups (small and large) over and over. I kept working my craft, which led me to being hired by Fortune 100 companies.

- Stop and look at the big picture. In order to see the 101 things you have to be good at, you need to take a break. What percentage of time a week do you run on autopilot? If you are like most workers, it is often. You have a job to do, deadlines to meet, and an executive to please. Commit to taking breaks at least once a day to see the big picture of the projects, tasks, and action items you touch or need to touch. Then even see beyond those to what others might expect of you and how various pieces connect.

■ Create processes that work and stay with you until something better comes along. The first step is to find processes that work for you because then you will be more apt to stick with it. There are many good processes available today but if you will not stay with them because they're not in your DNA, then don't use them. For example, while there are several digital apps or tools for tracking 'to do' items and follow-up items, I find my very best follow-up system is still the 43-hanging file folder system. It never fails me. By the way, there are solid processes for every major task you must do as an assistant. If you want to learn what star executive/assistant partnerships do for processes, purchase my *Executive and Assistants Working in Partnership: A Definitive Guide*. You can obtain the Guide at www.OfficeDynamics.com.

■ Work efficiently. Two definitions of efficiently are: 1) in a way that achieves maximum productivity with minimum wasted effort or expense. 2) in a well-organized and competent way. If you do something efficiently you do it productively and quickly. That makes good sense because assistants have a plethora of tasks and assignments thrown at them. When I was an assistant, I was not a big chit-chatter; I had way too much to get done in my contained 40-hour week. That's not to say I never worked over 40 hours because I certainly did. Times are different and you actually have more challenges because of technology distractions. You have IMs popping up in your face; social media news; your kids or partner texting you; and possibly an open-office environment. Therefore, you have to consciously work at being efficient.

- Focus. I will never tire of talking about being focused. If you have been a follower of me for a long time, you know how I feel about the importance of focus. This ties somewhat into the previous bullet-point idea. This is where you can really stand out and shine. The ability to focus is a skill. It is a skill that requires practice and conscious attention. I strongly urge you to develop this skill. It will help you in your professional and personal life.

- Do tasks that you don't necessarily like to perform. As an assistant, you are required to wear many hats and fulfill many functions. I didn't always like some of the things I had to do when I was an assistant, especially assignments involving numbers or mundane tasks. But I did them anyway because I knew that was what great assistants did and they did it without complaining. In today's business climate, you have to be versatile, flexible, and adaptable. And you must always keep yourself marketable.

**WHAT NOW?**

As a result of reading this chapter, what action steps are you going to take in the next 30 days to move in the right direction?

1. _Update print Sched._ _____

   _____

2. _____

   _____

3. _____

   _____

**WHAT OTHER THOUGHTS COME TO MIND?**

_____ _Share my Print Map_ _____

_____

_____

# CHAPTER 2

# THE NEXT BIG SECRET— BELIEVE!

WHILE DOING 101 THINGS well is vital to being a star assistant, your thinking is at the core of your success. Change your thinking and you will change the trajectory of your life. In other words, you can have all the skills in the world but if you can't be mindful, use positive affirmations, prophesize, and see success, you will not achieve the heights available to you.

Each and every one of us has untapped potential. This is a special gift and birthright. It's whether we choose to tap into ourselves and challenge ourselves that makes the difference in stellar assistants. But let me be clear on what I mean when I say success. Success is not always about moving up. Success is about expanding yourself where you are currently planted. In our premier training program for assistants, the Star Achievement Series®, we talk about belief as an important first step to achieving goals.

The course workbook says, "Belief is an important first step to reaching goals. You have to believe you can reach your goal or accomplish a task for it to happen, because that belief will get you through the tough times and help you overcome barriers. And there will be barriers to reaching your goals; there will be tough times—you can count on it! Anyone who has done anything worthwhile, served others, or conquered barriers, knows there are difficulties along the way, but it is their belief in what they want to do that keeps them going."

> *Believe in yourself!*
> *Have faith in your abilities!*
> *Without a humble but reasonable confidence in your own powers you cannot be successful or happy.*
> —NORMAN VINCENT PEALE

Your belief system is the catalyst to career accomplishment and personal satisfaction. It is the foundation on which everything else in this book builds. Your belief system has to be so strong that doubtful peers and friends don't rattle you. Their fears and pessimism must not get in the way of making your dreams become a reality.

## WHAT NOW?

As a result of reading this chapter, what action steps are you going to take in the next 30 days to move in the right direction?

1. _Stay positive_ _____

   _____

2. _____

   _____

3. _____

   _____

## WHAT OTHER THOUGHTS COME TO MIND?

_Some success due to others believing in me — N. Schmidt, B. Fischer Etc._

# CHAPTER 3

# PERCEPTION IS A FUNNY THING

**NEXT LET'S TAKE A** serious look at your perceptions of yourself, your role, and your life. Your perceptions are important because they can become your realities. In other words, if you perceive that you should work independently, make decisions, and be a part of the management team, you will behave in that fashion. If you believe your job is to take specific direction, do only what you are told, and not stretch into new territory, that is what you will do.

A big secret to my administrative success is that I saw myself as a business partner. I expected respect at every level I worked, including my first receptionist position. If I did not feel respected, I left the job or the company. My confidence may have come from the fact that I had incredible parents who always made me feel worthy and good as a human being. My parents were uplifting even when life was really hard. My dad was an entrepreneur and owned his own business. He was confident and strong and my mother … wow … for that day and age, my mother was an immensely strong and bright woman. I'm not sure about your past but I hope you, too, had positive role models.

In addition to your personal perceptions, there are the perceptions that others form of the administrative profession based on what they see those in the industry doing and portraying. What do I mean? Simply that when a publisher or a company uses cutesy images to portray assistants, they belittle the profession. They send a message to those viewing that article, blog, or Facebook post that this profession is not for grownups. I am upset by this as I have been trying for 40+ years to elevate this profession. I have personally put in years of portraying this profession as a career of choice and one that should be respected at all levels. So, do you see the problem? One group of people (me and a few others) who are trying to uplift the profession are going one way and the other group of people (who mean well) are going in the other direction.

What does this have to do with you? After all, you can't control others, correct? But you can control how you choose to portray yourself within the profession. You can choose how you walk, talk, act, and communicate. You have the power to write in a professional manner. You can make a difference. I have always believed in the 'Power of One.'

Let's take a step back for a moment. I want you to stop reading this book, close your eyes, and answer "How do I see myself? How do I view myself in this profession?" Now open your eyes and answer these questions:

- Do I like what I perceive? *O-K.*

- Am I living what I perceive? *yes*

- Am I truly living up to my highest potential? *always strivin*

- What messages am I sending to others in the workplace through my actions, speech, and reactions? *get it done fits fa a way*

- What impression am I giving with my email signature line? Am I using cutesy images and icons?

- Do I view myself as a business partner? *yes*

- What am I willing to do to help shape other people's perceptions, in a positive way, of the administrative profession?

Here's the big secret. Let's go beyond perceptions of your role. You need to see your life as a big picture, a full picture. Don't be so microscopic that you don't see how all the pieces of your life fit together. Because your work is not the only thing about you, even though you spend 40+ hours at work or working (in case you work remotely). When you look at your career as a piece of the bigger picture, you will rise far above thousands.

When I wrote my book for women called *Give Yourself Permission to Live a BIG Life*, I introduced the 5 Pillars of Life: Career, Family, Financial, Spiritual, and Wellness. I will talk about the 5 Pillars a bit later in this book and you might want to get a copy of *Give Yourself Permission to Live the BIG Life* from www.OfficeDynamics.com.

---

## WHAT NOW?

As a result of reading this chapter, what action steps are you going to take in the next 30 days to move in the right direction?

1.  _____

   _____

2.  _____

   _____

3.  _____

   _____

---

## WHAT OTHER THOUGHTS COME TO MIND?

_____

_____

_____

# CHAPTER 4

# CHOOSE TO GROW

**NOW THAT WE HAVE** covered perceptions (in Chapter **3**), let's talk about growth as a choice. You choose to grow. You choose to commit to whatever it takes to grow. We can't grow and be stagnant at the same time. It's not humanly possible. But to reinvent doesn't mean to throw everything out! It means to honestly explore what works really well for you and keep it and identify what is holding you back and get rid of it! Whether it is the words you say, actions you take, clothes you wear, annoying habits, old-fashioned thinking, or the friends you hang around with—change it!

You must reinvent yourself. You will do this again and again throughout your career.

*You need to have a larger sense of 'self' that transcends the 'I am just an Admin' mentality.*

This really says it all. If you want to change the way people view you and be taken seriously, be seen as part of the management team, gain respect for your ideas and your persona, then you have to act in a way that demands it. Your actions and speech will stem from the thoughts going on inside your head. If you think, "I am just an admin with limited authority," then you are right. If you think, "I am a positively powerful being who is a strategic partner to all of management and I can be a driver of change," then you will live that out, with ongoing personal and professional development.

If you choose growth, a good first step is to identify the skills and attributes necessary to succeed in the administrative profession—not just have a good career but really exceed and succeed. Following that, you can objectively assess your current performance and set stretch goals for areas of growth.

## Discipline and Consistency

John Maxwell, world renowned thought leadership expert says, "Motivation gets you going; discipline keeps you growing. Consistency is doing the right thing every day whether you feel like doing it or not."

Choosing growth means you have a thirst for knowledge. Being hungry for knowledge is different than being hungry for information. You can get all kinds of information and never become knowledgeable.

There are three levels of learning/knowledge access for you:

1. Peer-to-peer learning is what I call the basic or foundational level. This is when you get ideas from your administrative peers. This is when your assistant friends teach you shortcuts and new ways of doing things.

2. Senior assistants is the next group you want to access. When you learn from high-level executive assistants, this is considered advanced learning. Unless you are the top-level assistant in the organization, there is an executive assistant who is higher up the ladder. These seasoned executive assistants have a great deal of smarts or they would not be working for the top dogs in the company. Do not be afraid to reach out to these assistants.

   I will never forget Margaret. A lovely, magnificent executive assistant who helped me a great deal when I got my first job in a big corporation in Cleveland, Ohio. It wasn't my first job; it was the first in a huge corporation. The company owned JoAnn Fabric stores across the country, and I worked at the corporate office. I was in my early 20s and Margaret was probably in her 40s. I looked up to her, I admired her, and she was a true mentor. Margaret took me under her wing and we became very good friends.

3.  The next level you must aspire to is what I call the master level of learning. That is when you step outside of your profession and your world and learn from a variety of thought leaders on a range of topics. This is when you learn from people like Sheryl Sandburg, Daren Hardy, Les Brown, and Simon Sinek. Are you saying, "Who are those people?" Good. That means you have some homework to do.

    At this level, you should at least occasionally read the *New York Times*, *Wall Street Journal*, *USA Today,* and *Inc. Magazine*. You might even pick up an industry-specific periodical or trade journal.

I started doing this at a young age so I am not asking you to do anything I have not done or that I continue to do. This secret alone will push you miles ahead. This master level of learning should excite you. Be ready for something very strange and wonderful to happen. You will realize that the more you know, the more you don't know. And you will become eager to learn more about our big wonderful world.

**WHAT NOW?**

As a result of reading this chapter, what action steps are you
going to take in the next 30 days to move in the right direction?

1. _Darren Hardy Daily_ _____

_____

2. _____

_____

3. _____

_____


**WHAT OTHER THOUGHTS COME TO MIND?**

_____

_____

_____

# CHAPTER 5

# WHAT MAKES YOU STAND OUT?

**CAN YOU SUCCINCTLY ANSWER** this question in **10** seconds? If not, you have some homework to do.

Since 1990 I have been preaching to assistants to be star achievers. What is a star achiever? An individual who continually strives to reach for the stars; to be their best; an individual who is on a lifelong journey of growth and excellence. What does it take to be a star achiever? A strong combination of attitude, skill, teamwork, and strategy. I came up with this formula when I started Office Dynamics and I was deciding what I wanted to teach assistants. I looked back over my 20 years' experience in the field and business world and asked myself, "What made certain assistants stand out where others did not?" That is how I got to my answer.

I would like to dissect this idea of standing out because I know when some assistants hear this they don't think standing out is a good idea. Other assistants think it is prideful to stand out. Others are embarrassed if they do not blend in. I have even had a participant in a class tell me when she was raised, her father told her to not do anything that would bring attention to herself (even if it was positive). How sad is that?

There is a beautiful quote by Marianne Williamson that I would like to share with you.

> *"Our deepest fear is not that we are weak. Our deepest fear is that we are powerful beyond measure. It is our light, not our darkness that most frightens us. We ask ourselves, who am I to be brilliant, gorgeous, talented, fabulous? Actually, who are you not to be? You are a child of God. Your playing small does not serve the world ... As we are liberated from our own fear, our presence automatically liberates others."*

Fortunately, as a young assistant, I did not have the fear of showing my talents and capabilities. I knew I had to demonstrate what I could do so I could obtain better positions and eventually land that job working for a CEO. I purposely sought opportunities to be visible but not in an egotistical way. My goal was to advance myself doing things or taking on projects that helped either my executive, department, or the company. My intent was to be a blessing to others and make their lives easier. Do you see why standing out can be a good thing?

Since owning my business and having my own employees, I have purposely looked for the strengths in each person. I purposely observe my employees to see what gifts they have that I can utilize. My goal is to leverage their talents within the organization because they will be much happier employees doing what they love and Office Dynamics will win.

Anyone can be ordinary or do ordinary work, but you were not born to be ordinary. There is no one on this planet who is like you, who thinks like you, looks like you. You are designed for greatness but you must do the work.

Think of standing out as the icing on the cake. When other assistants are just as good as you and have as much experience as you, what gives you the edge? Why would I select you to be on my team over another highly qualified assistant? What would make me want to retain you as my executive assistant vs. looking for someone else?

There are a few ways to determine your gifts. One way is to think about what you like to do at work. Do you love organizing the office and projects? Do you like helping people? Maybe you like working with detailed information or numbers. What about planning events or corporate meetings? Are you good at travel planning? Next, look at the skills required to do that particular task. It isn't so much about the travel planning as it is about ...

- Coordinating multiple facets of a trip

- Communicating in a way that makes that trip flawless

- Strategically thinking out the entire trip from the time your executive leaves home to the day he or she returns home

- Being creative

Do you see those are your gifts? Then you can seek other tasks or projects or new endeavors at the office that utilize those skills. This is the secret.

Another way to learn about your gifts is to talk to people who know you well in the business world. Ask them what talents they see within you. How would they describe you?

You also have to try new things to see what lies within you. One executive assistant, Jasmine, worked with me for ten years. On the day she departed Office Dynamics, she was a very different, talented person from the person who showed up her first day of work. In the early years, I would ask Jasmine to write articles, blogs, and hop on video with me or do a Facebook live. Jasmine always said yes. She was always willing to try new things. Over time she became quite comfortable and loved it.

My current team is an awesome group of individuals. Each has special gifts and talents. My assistant, Melia, is wonderful with people—she loves to help people and takes the time to talk to them or write them with the information they need. She is very warm and caring. Our executive clients and assistants love Melia.

It's really important that you figure out your strengths and natural gifts so you can be a blessing to yourself and others.

## WHAT NOW?

As a result of reading this chapter, what action steps are you going to take in the next 30 days to move in the right direction?

1. _____

   _____

2. _____

   _____

3. _____

   _____

## WHAT OTHER THOUGHTS COME TO MIND?

take it one step further

deliver it

# CHAPTER 6

# SEE YOURSELF AS A STRATEGIC PARTNER

**YOU HAVE HEARD IT** a hundred times: You don't work 'for' someone. You work 'with' someone. That is the way it should be. Do you truly feel like you are a business partner with your executive? Are you included in the decision-making process? Do you attend your leader's staff meetings and do more than just take notes? Does your leader take you seriously?

Fortunately, I learned this at the young age of 26. At the time I was working in a large corporation called TRW in Cleveland, Ohio. My executive, John, was Vice President of Marketing and Planning for TRW Automotive Worldwide. John was bright, enthusiastic, and creative. He had tons of energy and it was not unusual for him to be in the office until all hours of the night or to come in on the weekends. (Remember, at that time, we did not have email and the technology we have today.) John traveled internationally and when he was in town, he was running from one meeting to another.

The one trait I truly valued and loved about John was that he always made time for me. He made me feel like I was the most important person in the 26-person department. I even came before the Directors who reported to him. John taught me about morning huddles and how to be a strategic partner to him. I worked with John for almost three years and then he was moved to another part of the company. I wasn't too excited about the gentleman who was taking his place, so I accepted a position in another company.

After I left TRW, I took what John taught me everywhere I went. Anytime I started working with new executives, I taught them how to be my strategic partner. I taught them about morning huddles and why they were important to our success.

Since 1990, when I started my training company, I have been teaching assistants and executives how to build strategic partnerships. If you want to truly learn how to function in partnership with your executive, purchase the operating manual I wrote, along with Chrissy Scivicque, called *Executives and Assistants Working in Partnership: The Definitive Guide*. You can purchase the Guide at www.OfficeDynamics.com.

For now, I will give you some key points on building a strategic partnership.

## Learn what's important to your leader.

- <u>Pay attention to details</u> – observe your executive's actions, behaviors, even attire. One assignment I have given assistants over the years is to keep a style diary of their executives. I tell them to really pay attention to their executives' work style, thinking style, how they approach problems, how they react to challenges, and really listen to what they say. You will learn a great deal about your executives if you just pay attention. This will lead you to understand them at a deeper level so you can build a stronger partnership with them.

- <u>Listen closely</u> – executives drop clues all the time. A long time ago I had an assistant and I would say, "This is important." She sometimes ignored what I said. She didn't take it as really important even though I had said it was important. When in doubt, ask your executive to identify their top priorities.

## Help Your Leader Look Great

- Be an outstanding office liaison (concierge). When I was an assistant, I had hundreds of opportunities to be the bridge between visitors and my executives. It was up to me to recommend great hotels for their stay; provide the names of the best restaurants; recommend town car services; and inform them of local events. I took the initiative to personally check out local providers of these services. Sometimes I took the word of my executive or other executives, but there were times they didn't think about what the room looked like at the local hotel or whether it had been renovated in the past ten years. The secret is to prevent any embarrassment to your executive because of your recommendations.

- Anticipate (and act on) challenges. Recognize what might make your leader look bad or embarrass him or her. Make it go away!

- Know who's who. Who is important to your executive inside and outside the organization? Executives sometimes refer to people who are important to them as key stakeholders. Keep your executive informed of any news you read or see about these people or their companies.

## Be a Valued-Added Partner

"Robots need not apply!" In my groundbreaking book, *Become an Inner Circle Assistant,* I wrote about being a cognitive being. You are more than an order taker and task doer. You have brains and you need to engage them throughout your day. Let me make my point through a story.

In all my training sessions, attendees are set up in teams. We usually have five people to a table and five tables in the room. Throughout the day, the teams work on activities, brainstorm ideas, and then report back to the entire class. Often, I set a time for an activity, let's say twenty minutes. Every once in a while I get a team who repeatedly finishes ahead of the others. You might say … these administrative assistants are sharp! If you guessed their speed was a result of their keen abilities … you would be mistaken. The other groups really massaged their assignments while this ahead-of-the-pack group used 'top of the mind' thinking to find their answers. They stayed in the shallow end … didn't dig deep. In short, they probably could have done better if they remained *engaged* in the matters at hand. Instead of remaining focused on assignments, they spent time chatting amicably.

The big secret is to dig deep, engage every sense throughout the day, and don't just work the surface.

Understand the scope of your executive's work. This is not the same as what your executive does such as budgeting, hosting meetings, or sales. These tasks don't represent the 'big picture.' I will use myself as an example to explain the scope of work. You might think the scope of my work is conducting workshops, speaking at conferences, writing books, blogs and articles, producing educational videos, coaching executive and assistants, and hosting an Annual Conference for Administrative Excellence. That is not correct. Those are the vehicles I use to achieve my scope.

## The scope of my work is to:

- Bridge the gap between management and administrative staff

- Be the visionary in the administrative profession and lead assistants and their executives to heightened levels of awareness as to how to work better

- Improve the quality of work life for assistants

- Make every assistant who attends our conference or courses feel like a VIP

- Increase awareness that the administrative profession is a career of choice

- Maintain being the leader in administrative training and producing the highest quality educational programs, products, and services for administrative professionals and their executives

Do you see the difference? I hope so because this is a big deal! If you can learn the scope of your executive's work, you will be much more valuable to your executive; you will take your work to an entirely new level and be recognized as a star in the profession.

To learn the scope of your executives' work, ask them. You want to know the deeper purpose of why they do what they do; why they work the long hours; why they are passionate about their work. Another way to learn about the scope is to really listen to your executive throughout the day. Again, listen at a deeper level. Listen to the words they use, the phrases, and the topics. Be aware of what really piques their interest. What do they seem excited about? What lights them up?

Another way to demonstrate your worth is by taking the initiative and doing little things that have a big impact. For example, when your leader travels to a place where an industry-related convention is in town—should she attend some sessions? It may be an ideal networking opportunity for her. Find out. In fact, as I was writing this book, I was on a flight to Columbus, Ohio, scheduled to teach my World Class Assistant professional designation course at Nationwide Insurance in Columbus. However, because of my Director's initiative to seek greater exposure for me while in the Columbus area, an arrangement was made for me to also speak to about 100 assistants at Ohio State University. This was a little thing that will have big impact.

## Understand their style/How they operate

We all know and have heard the word 'style' for years, particularly in terms of personality. There are all kinds of assessment tools such as DISC® to identify particular styles. Since 1990, I have been using a tool for discovering communication style preferences.

However, in this instance, I am referring to style in a different light. When I say style in terms of your executive, I mean the way one approaches problems, one's philosophy, feeling about the organization, reactions to others, general work habits, likes and dislikes, peak time of day, and hot buttons. This is another area where you need to be cognitive and fully engage your senses. To fully understand your executive's style, you have to observe, listen, be fully present, and pick up on nuances. You watch every little thing he does to learn his likes and dislikes like. Listen for his philosophies about work and life. What are his beliefs about coloring in the lines?

I will never forget the first great executive I supported. Pay attention ... he was not the first executive I worked for ... he was the first *great* executive I worked for. His name was John. We worked at TRW in Cleveland, Ohio. I have spoken of John many times in my career and in my other books. He had a tremendous impact on me as a young secretary that has carried me through to this day. John was a top executive, very sharp, smart, and charismatic. He was admired by both men and women in the organization. He was also a rebel. He did not color in the lines. John pushed the envelope, crossed barriers, and shook things up. He went against the grain but in his charismatic way so people didn't get angry. My understanding of his style helped me better support him, be his gatekeeper, and right-hand strategic partner.

## Keep in mind the following goals

Create a partnership that works—regardless of the 'players.' Sometimes we get to choose the executive we support. Occasionally, we are 'given' other executives or managers to support in addition to our key executive. And other times, our executive leaves and we are given someone else. That has happened to me. Regardless of the players, make it work. Unless you really cannot tolerate working for a particular person, just play to your audience. It's like me, as a speaker. I can have 20 – 500 people in an audience. I don't always choose who is in my audience. Because I am a professional at what I do, I accommodate just about everyone. If you work with someone who has a challenging personality, look for areas of agreement. Also, can you find a way to complement his style?

Another example of 'play to your audience' is when I worked at Schering-Plough in Memphis, Tennessee. I supported the VP of Marketing for Coppertone. (Yes, the Coppertone suntan lotion. It was a great job.) I was 17 years into my administrative career. My executive, Steve, was a young hot shot: very social, fun, and smart. He rarely stayed in his office. He managed by walking around and talking to his Directors. After being there awhile, I wanted to talk to him about providing higher partitions for the assistants. Our desks were close with low partitions and it was so noisy and distracting that it made it hard for me to work. Knowing Steve was a very social, laid back guy, I asked if we could go to lunch. At lunch we talked about his kids, family, and flying lessons. We were enjoying general conversation. Then I approached him with my request for higher work station partitions and explained why they were necessary. Do you see how I played to my audience? You will win more people over by playing to their needs first.

Develop a partnership in an atmosphere of trust and collaboration. Trust is critical in building a strong relationship. Your executive must trust you 100 percent and I don't just mean trust you with confidential information. In fact, it's more about them trusting you to get the job done, not drop the ball, follow through, and make them shine! Collaboration is different from teamwork. I highly recommend you Google the differences. With your executive you actually want teamwork *and* collaboration. Let's focus on collaboration as you probably are not aware of what it entails. In collaboration, there is no leader! So just because your executive is above you in status (and always remember that), you are a partnership. In a true partnership, you collaborate. You figure things out as you go along. You may change the course of action and run with things on the fly.

## Initiate communication

**I cannot express enough the importance of this! Do not wait for your executive to initiate conversation and spit out demands at you. Please remember and implement the following:**

- Everyone has a demanding schedule every day. You have your own schedule and list of things to do and so does your executive. You need to make time for purposeful conversation. This is where you discuss beyond the task; you dig deeper. For example, instead of just asking about an upcoming meeting, you talk about exactly what is required for that meeting, what is the impact or importance of that meeting, who are the players? What do those players mean to your executive? Is your executive completely prepared? What is the Plan B? The list goes on and on.

- You must have human moments. Human moments mean talking face-to-face or on the telephone. I often ask assistants if they talk to their executive and they tell me, "Sure. All the time. We email each other." That is NOT what I mean. Nothing will ever, ever replace human moments (with any person). Stop following the crowd and grow some courage! If you and your executive are to have a true partnership, you must talk to each other. And not just about your daily tasks. Remember I said you are not just a task doer and order taker. You have brains. Use them! For twenty years as an assistant, I had daily huddles with my executives (or at least 90 percent of the time).

As an executive and CEO since 1990, I have held daily huddles with my assistants and key team players. Nothing will ever replace the face-to-face or talking on the telephone. Often it is a lot faster than sending emails back and forth. When you have human moments, you instantly clarify what you thought you heard or what you thought the assignment was.

In human moments, you can challenge your executive's thinking. Often your executives are their own worst enemy. I know because I do it to myself. I will block out quiet time so I can write and then I will give it away. In a human moment, my assistant will say to me, "Remember, you need time to write. You will be angry at yourself if you give that time away." Human moments are where we build connections. It's where we build friendships, understanding, patience, and so much more.

■ Be concise and know what you want to say. Executives are very busy people. They don't have a lot of time. They are time compressed. Know what you need to say before you approach them, and then say it. They don't have time for you to be wishy washy or non-assertive. For me, I don't need the backstory. Just tell me where this situation or task is right now. Think about your own schedule and work. I bet you often feel overwhelmed. Now multiply that answer from 2 to 10 times and that is your executive's life! Don't take it personally when they don't have time for chit chat. The big secret is to use emotional intelligence and pay attention to when your executive wants you to move on and when he or she is in the mood to talk. This is what sets the super-achiever assistants apart from others. They pay attention.

■ Be prepared. You should always keep a running list and/or folder of what you need to discuss with your executive so that when you get her attention, you are ready to go. Your highest priority items need to be at the top of your list in case the conversation gets cut short.

■ Be a critical thinker. You are supporting management. This is a big deal. You are running their lives and that is a big responsibility. I highly recommend you learn about critical thinking.

## Teach your executive how to work with you

In my early days as a secretary I didn't know how to teach my executives how to work with me or what I needed. However, at a young age and because of my great experience with John G. (whom I wrote about earlier), I learned how a strategic partnership should work and I taught every executive after that how to work with me. You are reading this book and have access to volumes of information on how executives and assistants should work together. You are armed with tons of information I did not have at first. Basically, you have no excuse. Study, learn, and communicate with your executive. You are a business partner. Business partners want each other to succeed and want to operate at the optimum.

- Ask for challenging assignments. Sometimes executives just don't think to give you a challenging assignment. Or often they are thinking about the time they will have to spend to teach you. I'm here to tell you, I often asked my executives to give me more, teach me, and that I would handle it. This is a huge benefit to you because you grow your skill set. You become a more valuable asset because now they are relying on you for that task or piece of the project. It also keeps you from getting bored at work, which is the worst thing to happen!

- Maintain your processes even during busy times. You and your executive should have clear processes on every aspect of the typical tasks that need to be performed. For years I have coached executives and assistants how to implement processes on everything from daily huddles to debrief meetings, managing email, travel planning, and holding quarterly strategic meetings. As a result, I published an operating manual called *Executives and Assistants Working in Partnership*. The processes I spoke of then still exist today. They are great processes. What often happens is when work or business gets really crazy, processes get put aside such as regular huddles. That is when I notice, though, that most problems occur. So first you must have excellent processes in place and then, second, you stick with your processes. Or if you get off schedule because of heavy executive travel, you get back on schedule as soon as possible.

- Demonstrate what you can do for them. Don't always ask for permission. For example, maybe you can think of a better way to spruce up your executive's PowerPoint presentation. Don't ask if it's okay to change it, just change it. Show it to him. Let your executive see what you are capable of doing.

■ Communicate your desire to help and be a business partner. Don't wait to be asked to the party. Let your executive know you want to create this partnership and the benefits both of you will derive from doing so. Now not every executive or manager will want this partnership. If you support multiple managers, you won't have the time to build strategic partnerships with each of them. I can safely say, though, that today's progressive leaders want to have a partnership. They have a more modern approach which is the perfect opportunity for you to speak up.

## Model the behavior you want to see in your executive

In the mid-80s, my husband and I moved to Asheville, North Carolina. My husband, Dave, had received an excellent career opportunity. I was already 15 years into my career as an assistant. I knew how to be an executive's assistant. When we first moved to Asheville, I had a hard time finding a job that really suited me. Asheville is a very small town and there weren't many big businesses.

I tried a few different jobs and was never really fulfilled. Then I finally got an opportunity to interview for a great position as Executive Assistant to the GM of Steelcase North Carolina. I interviewed and got the position. My executive's name was John. Unfortunately for about eight years prior, John had an assistant who really didn't know how to be a great executive assistant. She performed at a basic level and just got done what was necessary. Then I came on board with 15 years of experience and I knew how to build a strategic partnership.

It took me one full year to teach John how we could have this amazing partnership and how I could be a huge asset to him. I modeled the behavior I wanted to see in him. In other words, I was open and honest; John eventually learned to be open and honest with me. I would write little notes to him on Post-its® with "Great job, John!" and eventually John would tell me, "Great job, Joan." Little by little I shared some personal things with John regarding family and such. Before I knew it, John was sharing some information about his wife and family. Model the behavior you want to see.

## Demonstrate your worth and knowledge

Talk is cheap. You have to walk your talk. In today's business world, you have to constantly demonstrate your worth and knowledge. Business is moving too fast and as I said earlier, the situation changes in a heartbeat.

- Be accurate in your information. Most executives who have gotten to the top have gotten there because of logic and accurate information. In my case, if you are going to speak with me or try to persuade me or convince me about something, you better be accurate. Make sure you take time to gather facts.

Stay abreast of current trends and technology. This will truly give you the edge. We know for a fact that 90 percent of the skills executives seek in assistants are the soft skills or what we call interpersonal skills. Obviously, though, you will be highly admired for your technical skills. We have to use the technology to get our jobs done. I know many executives rely on their assistants to troubleshoot.

■ Do not settle for mediocrity; raise your own bar. Recently, an assistant in a class of mine had been with a big organization for a very long time. She couldn't understand why she did not receive a particular promotion within the company. After all, she had been there for decades, was a hard worker, was a great assistant, and even tried to mentor other assistants. Well, I found out the back story from some 'power to be' that she was aggressive and too bold in how she spoke to people. The idea is to be a star in the profession and continue to raise the bar. But you also must be very aware of how you communicate, approach people, speak, and act. You can be really outstanding and blow it because you don't understand the art of communication.

## Learn Executive Speak

This information is from a module in Office Dynamics' Star Achievement Series® flagship training program for assistants.

Do executives speak differently than administrative professionals? Yes, many of them do. If you want to establish the commonality previously mentioned with your leader and other members of the management team, you will want to be a student of 'executive speak.'

When you learn to communicate in a fashion that they like and regularly use, you will create a more synergistic relationship with the leaders in your organization. It will open the lines of communication and your leaders will view you more as a business partner. Developing this skill will also be beneficial when you interact with high-level executives outside your organization, community officials, Board of Directors, C-level executives, or even potential employers.

Consider this saying: *"Great minds talk about ideas, average minds talk about events, small minds talk about people."* Many executives, leaders, and managers will discuss topics, ideas and issues. They seek to solve problems and develop vision. They utilize sports analogies to describe and give definition, using word pictures with a punch to communicate concepts.

## Here are some insights into leader languages or executive speak:

- Use straightforward communication. (Don't beat around the bush.)

- Be precise and concise. Busy executives do not have much available time.

- Communicate big picture, abstract ideas. While details are important, many high-level executives think big picture. The way to do this is to stand above all the pieces of your work and look at the big picture, just like a puzzle. Instead of looking at each piece, you have a picture of what the completed puzzle will look like.

- Mirror words and phrases they use, such as:
  - » Analyzed
  - » Flawless execution
  - » Strategic
  - » ROI
  - » Holistic
  - » Alignment
  - » Get in the game
  - » Engaged in the business
  - » Synthesis
  - » Get into abstracts
  - » Forecasting

» Near-zero tolerance

» Trite ideas

■ Speak with intelligence, thought, and clarity.

■ Use a confident tone.

■ Be prepared (organize and prepare what you are going to say).

## WHAT NOW?

As a result of reading this chapter, what action steps are you going to take in the next 30 days to move in the right direction?

1. _____

_____

2. _____

_____

3. _____

_____

## WHAT OTHER THOUGHTS COME TO MIND?

_____

_____

_____

# CHAPTER 7

# DEVELOP AN ASTUTE ABILITY TO SEE THE FUTURE

**IT JUST SO HAPPENS** that during the writing of this book, I was reading a book called *How to Be Like Walt: Capturing the Disney Magic Every Day of Your Life*. I felt compelled to read this book since I would be working with assistants at Disney World in Orlando. I was so inspired by the story of Walt Disney that words cannot even express my feelings. I highly recommend you read this book as the life of Walt, his values, his beliefs, and the way he lived life will inspire you to live a rich life. You will learn about building rapport with people, being creative, leadership skills, and how to live with adventure.

One of Walt's greatest attributes was the ability to see the future — to see tomorrow. I loved reading this chapter of the book because for more than two decades I have been teaching assistants to be future focused. In fact, this topic is so important, one of the full-day classes in my Star Achievement Series® is called Future-Focused Star Performer. In that course workbook, I have a list of driving forces shaping tomorrow. During class, we discuss how those driving forces impact assistants. In class, we always have great discussions and aha moments.

When I talk about being future focused, I'm talking about looking out six to nine months and sometimes, even twelve months. Our future becomes our present quickly. Times and conditions change rapidly. You want to look to the future so you can:

- Better prepare for what the future will bring.

- Take steps to prevent undue stress.

- Stay on the cutting edge.

- Avoid conflicting schedules.

- Build a sustainable infrastructure.

- Plan in a more timely fashion.

- Block potential problems.

What can you look for? How can you see the future when it is in the future? There are ways you can somewhat predict the future or anticipate what might happen so you can prepare for it. Here are some ideas. You can look for:

- Changes in technology

- Business trends

- Budget changes

- Upcoming schedules, major business events, travel

- Corporate vision

- Cycles (within your industry, organization, community)

But don't just read or listen for changes that are taking place. You must go beyond that and think about how the trends and changes could impact you personally and professionally. As you learn about trends, industry, the economy and more, ask yourself these questions:

- Do any of these trends currently pertain to me?

- If yes, how do they affect me? Do I need to alter some old patterns?

- Could they affect my profession within the next five years?

- If yes, how can I prepare for that impact?

## How can you anticipate the future?

- You can anticipate the future by paying attention to the present. Often what is going on in the present will give you an indication of what could happen in the future. An example is I am working with an amazing client right now. It is a huge corporation and I am doing extensive training with their assistants. As of today, we have six sets of dates booked between April and September. My key contact just wrote me the other day asking to talk to me about a few other ideas. After reading what the possible new ideas could bring to me, I told my assistant that probably the current training/travel schedule is going to change and be ready to make changes as necessary.

- Visit the past. Often if we look at past trends or situations, as they are strong indicators of what the future will bring. That is why you should take time to think about a past event or events. Often, we move from one thing to the next at work and don't glance back or discuss what happened at yesterday's executives' retreat. Those conversations are important. Holding a debrief after a meeting, executive retreat, board meeting, or conference is important.

- Ask yourself how could this go wrong? An example in our office would be when we launched a revolutionary program such as my Learning at Sea. In 2017, I held my first course at sea. It was something I had dreamed about doing since 1990 and finally decided to take a risk. But first I had to think about the worst-case scenario, such as what if we don't get the number of people we need to attend this course? After all, there are guarantees I need to give the cruise line. My team and I discussed what might not go as we expected and identified our Plan B.

- Connect with people at work and find out what is going on in their world. This is especially helpful when you work in an office. Many coworkers and higher-ups know things you do not know. Just as you have a network of resources, so do your coworkers. Especially connect with people you do not normally talk to because they will bring a different perspective. You should always think of having a broader vision of what is happening than what is in your own little world.

- Be abreast of your industry sector. This is pretty straight-forward.

- Take advantage of quick conversations at the company café. Once again, be a good listener. Be interested when colleagues are talking to you. Ask them to tell you more. Even though it may not pertain to you today, it could be useful to you in the next six or nine months or even a year.

- Ask your executive what is on the horizon in his world. Most executives have a lot of ideas swirling around in their head about what they intend to do a year and even two years out. Get inside your executive's head. Let your executive know you are interested in his vision and what he will be working on in months to come.

## Create the Future

Don't just see and respond to changes and the future: create the future. Be a catalyst for change. That is one of my big life secrets. I love to be a creator of what I want to see in the world. And I did this many times as an assistant. Here are some examples of what I did during my administrative career:

- When I worked for the CEO of Boatmen's Bank in Memphis, Tennessee, I started a group for the executive assistants called Star Achievers. We met regularly and I also provided mini-training classes for them.

- At TRW in my early 20s, we did not have corporate fitness centers. We worked in a building which had an empty office space. I was able to set up Jazzercise classes for some of the women during lunch time and/or after work. I knew we needed to de-stress.

- When I worked at Steelcase in North Carolina, I wanted the assistants to get some meaty information to help them in their careers. I put in my own extra time and did not ask for one extra penny. I held mini-training sessions throughout the year.

- In 1990, we were living in Virginia Beach. I had just officially started Office Dynamics. I also wanted to create an informal organization for assistants who reported to CEOs, which I called Star Achievers. I did not want all kinds of official structure and boards and dues. I accomplished what I wanted. When we left Virginia in 1992, the group decided to stay together and continue what I started. To this day, the group is still together—of course with some changes in membership because of life circumstances.

> *"As you envision the future, be boldly optimistic. Preach optimism and inspire people around you with your positive view of tomorrow."*
> **–PAT WILLIAMS, AUTHOR OF, HOW TO BE LIKE WALT**

## WHAT NOW?

As a result of reading this chapter, what action steps are you going to take in the next 30 days to move in the right direction?

1. _____

_____

2. _____

_____

3. _____

_____

## WHAT OTHER THOUGHTS COME TO MIND?

_____

_____

_____

# CHAPTER
# 8

# CULTIVATE
# A HIGH
# TOLERANCE
# FOR CHANGE

**WENDE MORROW IS A** high-level executive assistant who lives in Las Vegas. She is the strategic business partner to the CEO of R & R Partners. R & R Partners has driven billions in revenue for destinations, hotels, transit, and utilities.

I first met Wende in 2016 when she attended our Annual Conference for Administrative Excellence. We had 450 attendees that year, but I will never forget Wende. She came up to me at the end of the event and told me how much she enjoyed our conference, what she had gained and much more. Wende was well dressed, confident, and had beautiful, long black hair. After our conference, Wende wrote a long email to Jasmine Freeman (who supported me then) and copied me. She was filled with ideas and thoughts about the profession and wanted to know how she could be a part of the future.

Wende also attended our 2017 conference and a few months later wrote this to me:

*As I reflect on the many things from the latest conference and the beloved Office Dynamics' webinars I've watched, the most common thread that sings to me the loudest both personally and professionally is CHANGE and how to deal with it.*

*As we all know too well, change is all too often huge, unexpected and most assuredly CONSTANT, never completely easy and seamless and discriminates to no one.*

*I am learning that change and disappointment at every age has its own challenges, but I am forever on the quest of kaizen (Japanese term for continuous improvement) to take the sting out of it and to make it a positive fruitful journey at every turn, no matter how daunting the road map looks at the beginning.*

*Along the lines of accepting change and making it your friend versus foe, I wanted to share a most splendid quote.*

> *"If the door closes, quit banging on it! Whatever was behind it, wasn't meant for you. Consider the fact that maybe the door was closed because you were worth so much more than what was on the other side."*
> **—ANONYMOUS**

I was quite adept at change in my early days as was evidenced by my twenty-year administrative resume. I worked in twelve different companies in five states. You might be thinking I couldn't hold a job or maybe I wasn't that good of an assistant. But that was far from the truth. I was a hungry, eager assistant. I wanted to move up quickly; I wanted to explore and go after good opportunities if they were presented to me. Some of my changes were circumstantial. I lost two jobs due to downsizing. And we moved a few times with my husband's career.

There were also many things going on in my personal life which gave me lots of practice in dealing with change. I have been in constant change since those days: personal and professional; large and small; major and minor. And some devastating experiences. I am thrilled to say I learned the skill of riding the wave of change and would like you to do the same.

We live in a world of influx. Business changes minute by minute now. If you think your company is the only one creating change, I'm here to tell you, it isn't. If you think your leader is constantly changing her mind, so is every other leader in every industry. I see and hear it every day. I live in it. If you do not learn to accept change, be flexible, and ride the wave of change, you will eventually drown.

I'm going to share with you my best strategies for dealing with change. I have been teaching them since 1990. They all work. Sometimes one strategy will work and other times you need to use a combination of strategies.

## Anticipate

- Guess where things are going, if you can.

- Keep your ears and eyes open. Know what is going on around you at work, in your community, with your family.

- Pay attention to national events, trends, and current news. These could affect your employer's industry, your profession, and your job.

## Prepare

- Gather relevant information. Stay informed.

- Make specific plans for the upcoming changes so you feel more in control. Be active, not passive.

- Play out various scenarios on paper. "If this happens, I will do …"

## Assess

- How do you feel about this change? Why do you think you feel that way?

- What happens to you physically when you think about this change? Do you tense up or feel a burst of energy?

- How this change, whether self-initiated or not, will impact the 5 BIG Life Pillars: career, family, financial, spiritual, and wellness. (Or which of these Pillars might the change impact the most?)

## Visualize

- Imagine yourself in the new situation. See yourself positively on the other side of the change.

- With change comes both danger and opportunity. See both but focus on the opportunity.

## Accept

- Don't fight change that is inevitable.

- Get on with your life; don't procrastinate.

- Do something that makes you feel good, something that gives you a sense of achievement.

- Learn to adapt as quickly as you can.

## Get Support

- Share your feelings with a trusted friend or family member, someone who will let you cry or laugh, and who will listen. People can't always give you the answers, but if they really listen, sometimes that is help enough.

- Look for someone who will encourage you, who can lift you up, inspire you, and spur you on.

- Read inspirational and motivational materials.

- If people offer to run errands or help in some other way, be open to assistance.

- Seek spiritual support.

## Hang Tough

- Visualize yourself with your feet dug deep in the sand while waves of change come over you. They get stronger and the wind blows harder. Finally, the calm comes and you are still standing. You have survived the storm of change.

- Be resilient.

- Don't play the 'victim' card. Say, "I am a victor over my circumstances." As Robert Schuller would say, "Tough times never last, but tough people do." Tell yourself that you are strong and you will endure.

## Go Easy on Yourself

- Don't be too hard on yourself when you are feeling down or can't adapt as quickly as you had hoped.

- Catch yourself doing things well and reward yourself.

- Take care of yourself. Enjoy outside interests and relationships.

- Focus on what's the best thing to do right now. Don't think about everything that has to be done.

## Keep the Best of the Old in Your Life

- Try not to make several changes at once. In other words, don't change careers, move, and get married (or divorced) all at once.

- Cherish the good things or people in your life as you move through change.

## Regularly Write in a Gratitude Journal

- Whether you are going through good or bad change, keep a gratitude journal on your nightstand. Each night before going to sleep, take two or three minutes and write about the things and people for which you are grateful. Even in the worst of times, you will find several things for which you are thankful.

- Purchase all types of journals; make journaling fun.

## Look at Change as an Opportunity to Grow

- Tell yourself, "I am just stretching right now."

- Be confident that you will return to your old comfort zone or you will find a new one.

- Tell yourself, "I have all the skills required to succeed."

## Purposely Change

- Make small changes occasionally to become more comfortable with change. Take a different route to work, change your seat at the dinner table, or sleep on the other side of the bed.

- If you have children, create small changes with them so they will learn to cope with change more easily.

> *"Change is like going on an expedition: It can be a trudge or a hike. Take it all in and enjoy the view or focus on the faults—it's absolutely a choice."*
> **—JULIANA STOCK, TECHNOLOGY EXECUTIVE**

**WHAT NOW?**

As a result of reading this chapter, what action steps are you going to take in the next 30 days to move in the right direction?

1. _____

_____

2. _____

_____

3. _____

_____

**WHAT OTHER THOUGHTS COME TO MIND?**

_____

_____

_____

# CHAPTER 9

# VISION

NINETY PERCENT OF THE assistants I know do not have a mission statement or vision statement. If you are going to be that stand-out assistant who is always on a journey of pursuing excellence, then you need a mission and vision statement. They will give you clarity to the current state you wish to live and a picture of what you want your future to look like and who you want to be. These will give you a sense of direction.

While your mission and vision statements go hand in hand, they are two very different pieces of content. Let's look at some definitions I found in a Google search.

- **Mission statement** concentrates on the present. It informs you of the desired level of performance.

- **Vision statement** concentrates on the future. It is a source of inspiration. It provides clear decision-making criteria.

Many people mistake vision statements for mission statements. The vision describes a future identity while the mission serves as an ongoing and time-independent guide. The mission describes why it is important to achieve the vision. A mission statement defines the purpose or broader goal for being in existence. A vision statement is more specific in terms of both the future state and the time frame. Vision describes what will be achieved if the individual is successful.

## Your Guiding Light

Your mission statement will keep you on track. We get so caught up in our day-to-day work and our personal lives that we forget our real purpose. Organizations usually have their mission statements posted where visitors and employees can see them. Many organizations will refer to their mission statements throughout the year. They are meant to guide the organization and everyone who works within that organization. It is the same for you. Reviewing or stating your mission statement often will help you stay the course. On the days you think, "What am I doing here? I wish I didn't have to work" … Your mission statement will remind you.

Your vision statement reminds you of who you want to be in the future or it can be a state of mind. When I first started as a secretary, my vision was to support a CEO in a large organization within "X" amount of years. It was my vision to support an executive at the top—the highest level. I could see myself being in that role … the excitement … the energy and challenge. By having that vision, I developed myself so I could be ready for that position. I networked with assistants and others who could help me achieve that goal.

Our vision gives us hope for our future. It tells us, "There is more to come. You are not done yet." Our vision can change and, I believe, we can have a vision for different aspects of our life. We can have a vision for our career and personal life or vision for our family life.

I'd like to encourage you to see writing a mission and vision statement as an interesting and fun assignment rather than drudgery. I know it may sound boring to you and like too much work. But I promise you that your mission and vision will help guide and steer you. Even if you can only jot a few words for each (mission and vision), that is a good start. Then you can build upon them later.

Here are examples of what assistants wrote in a Star Achievement Series® workshop:

**Mission:** Developing and enhancing our skills and relationships in a positive atmosphere while demonstrating the professional image that our company was founded upon.

**Vision:** Embrace the future empowered with new knowledge that encourages us to continue to grow.

## Impress Others

After you have written your mission and vision statements, you need to place them in your career portfolio. They should be placed up front, on nice paper, and typed in a professional-looking font. This way when others view your portfolio, they will quickly get a sense of who you are and where you see your future.

But don't stop there. You can place your mission and vision statements in a nice frame and place them at your work station. Imagine how impressed people will be when they see it. They will think to themselves, "Wow, this person really has it together!" Or, "She really knows herself and where she wants to be in the future."

I bet they will also be great conversation starters and give you a chance to let people know you at a deeper level. This is important if you want to be taken more seriously in the work place or considered for a promotion or larger assignments.

## Action:

Write your mission statement (the present)

_____

_____

_____

_____

_____

Write your vision statement (the future)

_____

_____

_____

_____

## Inspirational Vision

I just came up with this term but I have been living inspirational vision since I got out of high school. As an assistant, you have hundreds of opportunities in your career to inspire others with your vision for a better workplace and world. Inspirational vision plus painting the picture with words inspires others to join our cause. Assistants need people to join their cause personally and as an industry.

What might those causes be?

- Streamline processes. I am sure you see many ways in which the work around you can be streamlined. Whether that streamlining involves you and your executive or you and a team of administrative peers, you must be able to persuade people to make changes.

- Create an administrative team or community. Assistants need to collaborate and work in a more formal community to get greater visibility in an organization. When assistants gather together and create positive change for the organization, the view of the profession is elevated. I have always said it only takes one person to create change.

- Save the company money. In the 90s, Office Dynamics sponsored the Rising Star Award. It was an award for administrative teams who exemplified leadership, knowledge-sharing, and being a catalyst for change within their organization. We had a very stringent application process. In 1999, the administrative team at Dow Chemical Canada won the award for saving their company just over $1 million in less than 18 months! This was unbelievable that a group of 36 assistants could do this, but that demonstrates the power of good minds coming together, seeing the vision, taking ownership, and leading the charge. Imagine how your management team would feel about you and your peers if they accomplished something like this or even one fourth of this. And yes, the assistants were rewarded for their huge efforts.

- Get your organization to invest in onsite, administrative-specific training. This is not an easy mission, but several assistants accomplished this lofty goal and it started with just them! I can name several of these assistants right now. They are Joanne Linden (formerly with Synopsis), Debbie Gross (formerly with Cisco), Julie Reed (formerly with Huntington Bank), and Jill Wilhelm (formerly with Battelle).

And me! When I was an assistant I was able to convince my executives to let me hold training programs for our assistants. Granted, I was doing the training and that was partly because I knew someday I wanted to start my own training company. There was a strategy behind it, but I also sincerely believed assistants should be afforded great learning opportunities just as their executives were. I wanted to be the vehicle to bring rich, in-depth information to them. I was willing to do the hard work and put in personal time without extra pay or title change to make it happen. And I did.

The ladies I mentioned above all rallied to get the Office Dynamics' flagship training program, the Star Achievement Series®, into their organizations. That was not an easy sell because the Star Achievement Series® is a massive, in-depth training course consisting of twelve full-day workshops under three levels of learning. (We spread out the twelve days of training.)

So, what is your inspirational vision? What do you think needs to be improved or changed in your organization? Do you wish your administrative peers would be more open to sharing? Or what about hosting a fabulous event for your assistants during Administrative Professionals' Week? At the writing of this book, I learned that the assistants at Amazon were hosting their first big event called Amazon AdminzPalooza during Administrative Professionals' Week.

**WHAT NOW?**

As a result of reading this chapter, what action steps are you going to take in the next 30 days to move in the right direction?

1. _____

   _____

2. _____

   _____

3. _____

   _____


**WHAT OTHER THOUGHTS COME TO MIND?**

_____

_____

_____

# CHAPTER
# 10

# ELEVATE YOUR THINKING AND ELEVATE YOUR PAYCHECK

**IF YOU WANT TO** earn more money, you need to think differently, act differently, and sometimes even upgrade your appearance. It's so funny to me that people/employees think they should get a raise just because another year has passed. That is not the trend any more. In fact, many organizations are doing away with annual reviews. Instead they are giving employees pay increases as they are deemed.

Let's work with titles for a minute, just so I can make a point. Let's pretend that Suzanne is an administrative assistant and does a pretty good job. Suzanne has worked for an executive for two years and gets good reviews. However, at year two, Suzanne is wondering why she didn't get that much of a pay raise. What Suzanne doesn't understand is that while she did a good job all year, she didn't do much to develop herself or show an interest in learning what it takes to be a fantastic assistant. She expanded her job and took on new responsibilities but did not demonstrate the mindset of thinking at a higher level.

Disclaimer: Within organizations, there are set levels within a career path and usually salary ranges that match a career path. Therefore, there can be situations where the salary is dictated by the organization.

When I was an executive assistant in the mid-80s working for the General Manager (John R.) at Steelcase in Asheville, North Carolina, I had already been in the profession 15 years. I was an excellent executive assistant. The lady who was the prior assistant to the GM for 6 years never expanded herself or her job. She just did what was necessary. When I came on board, the General Manager entered a whole new world. It took me months, but I taught John how to utilize me as his business partner. I grew my position, took on new assignments, and demonstrated excellence. After six months, I felt I warranted a pay increase and a title change. My title was Staff Assistant because I supported the General Manager and his direct report staff. I felt that title did not completely represent who I was, who I supported, and the caliber of work I produced. I built my case (quite extensively), recommended a job title change, and requested a salary increase. John had to take my request to the corporate office in Grand Rapids as they set the structure. They approved my requests.

The big secret is you have to look, act, and speak the part of being at a higher level than what you are. This does not mean you have to move out of your position. It just means that if you want more, whether in pay increases, perks, or benefits, you have to expand your thinking and then demonstrate it.

This is why some assistants get a promotion when other assistants in the company do not. An assistant will say to me, "I don't know why she got that promotion. I should have." Well, it is because you are not demonstrating the thinking or behaviors to warrant it. I'm not saying that is always the reason but often it is and you will never know it.

## WHAT NOW?

As a result of reading this chapter, what action steps are you going to take in the next 30 days to move in the right direction?

1. _____

   _____

2. _____

   _____

3. _____

   _____


## WHAT OTHER THOUGHTS COME TO MIND?

_____

_____

_____

# CHAPTER
# 11

# SET STRETCH GOALS

**THE BROCHURE PROMOTING AN** administrative training program said, *We will never make you do anything you don't want to do.* Oh heavens, I thought! Really? How do you think a person grows? This was in a brochure from a company who hosts supposedly high-level classes for assistants. Pleeeaazzz!

Since 1990, I have been stretching assistants out of their comfort zones. I have asked them to write and give three-minute presentations; role play with participants; challenged them to think beyond the typical answer in class; project their voice; write difficult development plans; and even come up on stage with me at our Annual Conference for Administrative Excellence. And do you know what? As scared or nervous as they were, they stepped up to the plate and they were proud of themselves afterward. Do you know what else? They got promotions, salary increases, developed better relationships with their executives; they joined committees and chaired events; they set healthy boundaries; they gained immense confidence! That's what stretching can do for you.

Don't you dare settle for mediocre goals. You were not born to be mediocre. Staying in a comfort zone will eventually be your career death. Nothing great comes without discomfort.

What is a stretch goal? It is a goal that causes you to go beyond what you know. It is a goal that challenges your thinking and basically makes you uncomfortable. Please trust me on this one. It is okay to feel discomfort. Don't be afraid of it; rather, lean into it. I would not be where I am today professionally and personally had I not set stretch goals throughout my life. Do they hurt? Yes! Sometime you will want to scream and run away and say, "I don't want to do this." But if you stop or if you quit, you will never know the beauty that lies on the other side.

I will never forget when my husband, Dave, and I moved away from my hometown of Cleveland, Ohio. I had lived in Cleveland all my life. It was my home. I had a huge family in Cleveland and I loved growing up there. I met Dave Burge when I was working for Fabri-Centers of America in Cleveland. I was a secretary working at the corporate office in Cleveland and Dave reported to my boss. Dave lived in Minneapolis. He was a District Supervisor, who with all District Supervisors, reported to my boss and had to give me their weekly travel schedules. Yes, it ended up being an 'office romance.' For Dave and me, it was our second marriage. When we were married, I moved to Minneapolis where Dave lived. That didn't last too long as I was so homesick for my family in Cleveland. Dave was so in love with me, he gave up an awesome job and we moved to Cleveland where Dave worked for my dad's company. That lasted eight years, which was really long because Dave was ready to move away after a few years.

When we finally moved from Cleveland with our two little children, I was definitely out of my comfort zone. I had never lived away from family and Cleveland for any length of time. On top of it, we moved to South Carolina to live with Dave's parents for a while until we found jobs. Yep, we left Cleveland with NO jobs and two kids! The little old South was nothing like the big city I grew up in. I kept wondering, "Where are the disco clubs?" After several months of pounding the pavement every day, Dave found an amazing position and we moved to Asheville, North Carolina, where we lived and thrived for five years.

Over our 34-year marriage, Dave and I moved out of state eight times and lived in twelve different homes. I tried various jobs until I finally started my own company, which was definitely out of my comfort zone. Now that I reflect on my life, it seems that I have rarely lived in a comfort zone for very long.

The most incredible things happened to me over all those years of change and moving around. I met and still have very good friends in different states. My perspective of the United States broadened. My appreciation of diverse personalities, religions, cultures, and ethnicities has grown. I am confident traveling and going to unfamiliar places. I have incredible memories, many good times, many hard times, but most of all, I am eternally grateful.

Do you see I would know none of this if I didn't venture out? I would not be who I am today without all those experiences. I would not have tons of friends and a huge support group had we not moved around. Of course, I'm not saying you should move out of state. I am saying you have to move out of your comfort zone! You can do that right where you live and where you work. Go to lunch with new people. Take on a course that challenges you. Travel to Las Vegas and attend our fabulous conference and meet assistants from countries around the world.

The world is waiting for you—what are you waiting for?

**WHAT NOW?**

As a result of reading this chapter, what action steps are you going to take in the next 30 days to move in the right direction?

1. _____

   _____

2. _____

   _____

3. _____

   _____


**WHAT OTHER THOUGHTS COME TO MIND?**

_____

_____

_____

# CHAPTER
# 12

# BE A LEADER

## Self-Leadership Is My Big Secret

ANYONE CAN BE A leader. Leadership is not attached to a title but rather, leadership is a set of characteristics and that is why you can be a leader. In this chapter I will explore the characteristics of leaders, why you should want to lead, and how you can be a leader in your role. But first I want to talk about self-leadership.

Learning to lead myself (from a young age) was and still is one of my most powerful secrets. When you lead yourself, others will naturally follow. They will be inspired by your actions. They will see that you seem to manage life's challenges and crises better than the average person. You will project more confidence, therefore encouraging others to take bold steps.

**Career** Imagine if you move through your work day with a positive attitude and 'can-do spirit,' even when you are having a tough day. Co-workers, executives, and visitors will notice.

**Family** (Includes best friends and pets.) If you nurture family time, extended family members will follow. Your friends will notice the bond you have with each other and will want that connection for their family.

**Financial** If you pay off debt, save for your future, and manage your money, your life will be less frazzled. You will be able to ride the wave of economic changes.

**Spiritual** If you lead yourself spiritually—meaning you lead with your inner source, the real you—you will be more fulfilled, which energizes you and people will notice. Be authentic!

**Wellness** If you ride a bike, walk, or jog in your neighborhood on a regular basis, your neighbors will see you and some will be inspired to do the same. You will bring vitality to work and home.

If you have not read my book, *Give Yourself Permission to Live a BIG Life*, I highly recommend you purchase a copy and read it cover to cover. I have pinpointed areas of your life where you need to take the lead. In my book, I introduced the 5 Pillars of a BIG Life: Career, Family, Financial, Spiritual, and Wellness. I talk about giving equal attention to your 5 Pillars over a one-year period. I do not believe in nor use the word balance as many others do when they talk about their work and personal life. My Pillars are never in balance. One or two always get more attention at certain times than the other Pillars. It is almost impossible to think about balancing your Pillars and creates a ton of stress.

Leading yourself in the 5 Pillars is a good place to start practicing leadership and then amplify leadership specifically in your Career Pillar since we are talking about your role in the workplace.

*"Change your mind and you will change your life!
Lead boldly...shine brightly!"*
**—UNKNOWN**

## The Pillars are Interwoven

As you can see by the visual on the previous page, the Pillars are interwoven. While you focus on each one throughout the year, they impact each other. Some examples are:

<u>Financial fitness</u> helps physical wellness. You will be able to provide for your family and take them on that special vacation.

<u>Career</u> helps with financial, which means you can pay your bills, maintain your home, and support a local cause.

When we are <u>spiritually connected</u>, we operate at a higher level and experience more meaningful relationships.

Being connected to <u>family</u> (and not just blood relatives) is essential to a happy and healthy life.

Taking care of our <u>bodies</u> and fueling them with the right foods or activity trigger the 'happy' endorphins, which stimulate creative thinking and help manage stress.

Here are some tips to get you started in each Pillar. Again, I encourage you to read my book, *Give Yourself Permission to Live a BIG Life*.

## Career

- Remaining on a plateau is <u>dangerous</u>.

- Ordinary is easy. Extraordinary separates you from the crowd.

- Own your reputation. (If you don't have a strategy or plan for your reputation and brand, someone else will, or your brand will be known as vanilla.)

## Family

(Includes good friends and pets and maybe close friends at work.)

- Family is a stage for each member to express themselves.

- Relationships: What could we learn from each one?

- Support and love is a reciprocal happening, a two-way street. You give, you receive. You receive, you give.

## Financial

- Money in and of itself is not bad; it's what we DO with money that is good or bad.

- Dave Ramsey, the financial expert, says, "Spend every dollar on paper and give it a purpose."

- Women need to 'stick their noses' in finances, especially if they are married.

## Spirituality

- Spirit is courage, bravery, and resolution. Just like the eagle that soars in the sky, spirit helps us spread our wings and fly above our fears, obstacles, and doubts.

- Our spirit craves victory and growth. Our spirit is bold, strong, and adventurous.

- When you are in touch with your inner spirit, you feel energy because your body, mind, and spirit are united.

## Wellness

- Dr. Robert Michler says, "Our society has become so accustomed to <u>supersizing</u>, we take big for normal. We have to redefine normal. It's not normal to supersize everything. It's not normal to always take elevators and not walk."

- Allow into your awareness only feelings of strength, happiness, and success.

- Negative emotions can't survive in an environment of gratitude.

## Characteristics of Leaders and Managers

Since 1990, I have been encouraging administrative professionals to view themselves as leaders. The chart on the next page is actually in one of our Star Achievement Series® workbooks. I want you to see the descriptors for both leader and manager orientations. You should easily see the difference between the two orientations. As you read the list, maybe you can see which characteristics identify you. If you are not sure, then you do not favor one orientation over the other, which means you will have to work harder to grow the leader behaviors. If you fall heavily on the manager side, you will have to work even harder to develop the attributes of a leader.

| LEADER ORIENTATION | MANAGER ORIENTATION |
|---|---|
| Visionary | Task-oriented |
| Challenges employees to stretch | Keeps people in their comfort zones |
| Revolutionizes | Refines present things |
| Doesn't like stagnation | Strives to maintain the status quo |
| Optimistic | Pessimistic |
| Creates change | Values stability in the face of change |
| Creates a new culture | Preserves current culture |
| Focuses on opportunity | Sees danger |
| Provides inspiration, encouragement | Gives instruction |
| Empowers employees | Tends to be controlling |
| Thrives on crisis | Strives for stability |
| Has vision for overall purpose | Limits imagination and creativity |
| Favors unstructured approach | Prefers structured approach |

## Practical Application

Below is a starting point list for you. Then I highly encourage you to think of the many ways you can portray leadership in your organization.

- Manage projects, priorities, and daily tasks.

- Lead your executive to building a strategic partnership, thus increasing productivity.

- Professionally handle an office conflict.

- Reduce the number of emails you send.

- Be a strategic thinker.

- Pay attention to details  and ask questions.

- Keep an organized work area.

- Maintain calm when times are stormy (in the office or with the  business).

- Focus.

- Treat others the way you would like to be treated.

- Create peer synergy.

- Make timely decisions.

- Develop persuasion and negotiation skills.

## WHAT NOW?

As a result of reading this chapter, what action steps are you going to take in the next 30 days to move in the right direction?

1. _____

   _____

2. _____

   _____

3. _____

   _____

## WHAT OTHER THOUGHTS COME TO MIND?

_____

_____

# CHAPTER
# 13

# SEEK MENTORS

**MENTORS SAVE YOU TIME,** energy, and even money. They reduce stress and make life easier. Mentors challenge us to be our best, hold us accountable, and make us take a close look at ourselves which is not always easy. Whether you are at the beginning of your career, middle or end, you need a mentor. Regardless of your administrative title, industry or size organization, you need to find a good mentor.

## What to look for in a mentor?

You want to think about a mentor as someone who has already done what you want to do. Or someone who has behaviors, good habits, or attitudes you want to embrace. Let's say that you want to be confident presenting your ideas to others. You would look for an individual who excels in this area. Maybe you want to work your way into the C-Suite. You seek out an executive assistant who is working in the C-Suite and lives the qualities you admire. There are some people in the C-Suite you may want to model. I once knew a seasoned assistant who was nervous about going to lunch with other assistants and conversing. She really didn't know how to talk to other assistants and yet she wanted to do that. I mentored and coached her. I won't get into the differences between a coach and a mentor in this book.

## What to expect from a mentor?

I have been on both sides of mentoring. When I was an assistant, I had my own mentors. When I started getting in to the speaking and training business, I had several mentors. And since 1990, I have mentored several people professionally and personally. I believe a good mentor:

- Is transparent. A good mentor doesn't pretend or act like they are perfect. They are open and honest about their own mistakes and then openly share how they managed those and what they learned from them.

- Answers your questions. They have answers to your questions and usually can do it on the spot. They can quickly answer because they have years of experience; they know the ropes; they are confident in what to do. Now they may do extra research on the areas you two are focusing on but that is just bonus material. When I am coaching or mentoring, I provide all my insights from 40+ years in the workplace and the administrative profession. And usually I like to do some extra research to see what is current or new and recommend resources to my mentees.

- Holds you accountable. Mentors love to help and will mentor for free. In return, they expect the mentee to be serious about this relationship and make changes or execute ideas. You do not want to waste your mentor's time by chatting for an hour and then never implementing anything they recommend.

- Supports you emotionally. Sometimes life is a roller coaster. As we try to become better people or improve areas of our life, we can get a bit emotional about it. Even change we want is scary. When I left the administrative profession of 20 years and went into the speaking business and training industry, I was scared. And I needed someone to understand my fears and dreams.

- Uses emotional intelligence. A great mentor applies emotional intelligence especially the third dimension—using social awareness. That is when I adapt based on how you are feeling or acting. I am aware of your state of being and I adjust accordingly. I know when to push and when to back off.

- Maintains confidentiality. This is a very important trait as you will share your deepest wishes with this person; you might talk about your frustrations with your executive or peers or may talk about finances or family. You want someone you can count on 100 percent to maintain confidentiality.

## How to work with your mentor?

As I mentioned, your mentor's time is valuable and you do not want to waste your time either. You definitely should be prepared for any meetings with your mentor.

I make a list of my questions or thoughts. I write or type them in order of priority so if we run out of time, at least I got to talk about the most important items on my mind.

<u>Be clear on what you want from your mentor</u>. What kind of support do you need? What do you want your mentor to do for you?

<u>Communicate clearly and concisely</u>. If you know what you want and what you expect as a result of your meeting, you should be able to clearly and concisely communicate. However, some people are very chatty and carry on conversations twenty minutes longer than need be. Do not let this happen unless your mentor encourages it.

<u>Be respectful</u>. Your mentor is truly trying to help you. If you have chosen her because of her experience, then respect her ideas. You may not always agree but be respectful.

<u>Listen</u>. I know sometimes when I am being mentored, I am eager to hurry and express what I am thinking or even to explain why my perspective is not the same. I work at being quiet, taking in what my mentor is saying, and then commenting.

Keep an open mind. A good mentor should throw things at you that you don't agree with. There will be times you are going to think what they are saying is just plain weird and not buy into it. Be willing to try what they recommend. Give it some time. If it does not work for you, that is okay, but you can't judge that until you have given what they suggested sufficient time.

Thank your mentor. During discussions, be sure to thank your mentor for their ideas and their time. If you work with a mentor over several months, occasionally send him a hand-written thank you note. It will mean a great deal to him.

## WHAT NOW?

As a result of reading this chapter, what action steps are you going to take in the next 30 days to move in the right direction?

1. _____

_____

2. _____

_____

3. _____

_____

## WHAT OTHER THOUGHTS COME TO MIND?

_____

_____

_____

# CHAPTER
# 14

# SET AND KEEP
# YOUR BAR
# HIGH

**I HAVE ALWAYS HAD** high standards. Maybe that is because my parents were positive and expected great things in life. My dad never finished school, but he became a successful businessman, running his own company for 70+ years. When my dad was young, he always said he was going to own a Cadillac and have a nice home. My mother's parents came over from Sicily when my mom was three months old. I am fortunate that my grandparents wanted a better life by coming here and were able to provide even more for their children. So, my high standards go way back.

All through my childhood my mother told me, "Always do your best, Joan Marie. Whether you are making your bed or sweeping the floor, do your very best." And that is what I did. My mother always said this in a loving way and never with the intent of, 'We are better than others.' It was about being the best version of me. I have kept high standards all my life, whether I was an employee or owning my own business and in my personal life.

When Dave and I first moved to Asheville, North Carolina for his career, I had a very hard time finding a job. Remember, I was at the top of my field and now I moved to this very small town and I did not know anyone. Also, keep in mind I grew up and worked in a big city—Cleveland, Ohio. Casual dress had not arrived in the workplace yet. I finally got a job in Asheville as an Office Manager with a company called InterAct Computers. It was a small business with two small offices. Every day, though, I wore a skirt and top or something similar. I didn't wear my fancy business suits I had worn in Cleveland, but I did not wear jeans either, even though the other ladies in the office wore jeans. Do you know what happened after a few months of me being there? The other ladies upped their attire. They wore nice pants and nicer tops instead of t-shirts or sweatshirts.

I have always lived by the principle of 'Let people come up to my level. I will not stoop to a lower level in anything I do or in my appearance.' That takes a lot of courage. Learning not to follow the crowd is hard even for adults. Adults talk about kids and teenagers needing to fit in with their friends and yet adults act no differently. This happens often in the workplace. Everyone around you uses email to communicate regardless of the intent or situation. And so you consistently use email for your communications. Instead, you should be thinking about your goal and motive for communicating, your relationship to the person and then select the medium that will have the most impact. Do you see the difference?

Another example of keeping high standards is when I went to work at Steelcase in Asheville, North Carolina. We had 900 employees at that manufacturing facility. This facility is where we made beautiful real wood office furniture. We had 54 managers and 5 assistants. I worked with the General Manager of the division, thus holding the highest position.

Some background information first before I go on with my story. Prior to moving to Asheville, I had a 15-year administrative career. I always kept my nose to the grindstone when I went to work. I was not into a lot of chit-chat and social talk. I was very friendly and warm and would have casual conversations but most often I was there to do my job. I rarely took breaks. Then I arrived at Steelcase. If you know anything about the South, it is a slower pace, especially compared to a big city. It was not unusual for the assistants at Steelcase to stop and chat or go to coffee breaks a few times a day. Well, I was there to work. I had an immense job with the General Manager and supported five of his direct reports. I also headed up all client visits and tours of our showroom and managed the company jet. As a general rule, we were not supposed to work overtime.

After being at Steelcase for several months, one day the Human Resources Manager asked if he could speak with me. His name was Henry and he was a wonderful man. He was older and very kind. He commented—nicely—that some of the assistants felt I was a snob (those weren't the exact words he said) because I didn't socialize during the day. He thought since I reported to the top man, maybe I should chit chat a bit more. I told Henry I had a job to do and that is why they were paying me. However, I would compromise, so I planned monthly dinners for the assistants and myself. This was a time where I could relax and let my hair down and have the time to visit with them.

## A Problem with Today's Standards

I was fortunate to conduct a training for Sandals Resorts a few years back. The head of the corporate university was (and still is) a very wise man. I will never forget what he said to me on the phone one day. He talked about how employees believe they are operating at a higher standard but the problem is the standard has been lowered! Wow, that blew my mind. He hit the nail on the head. It is true.

People believe they are operating at a very high standard but over the years, the standard has been lowered. People have become more relaxed, casual, and nonchalant. People are less courteous and respectful. People confuse hard work with excellence and that is not necessarily true. You can work very hard and put in a lot of hours, but it does not mean you are approaching your work with excellence.

Whose standards are you following? Are you sure they are the right standards? This is where you have to be careful, thoughtful, and follow your own path. To help you determine which standards to follow, look to the top people in your organization. Surely there is a reason why they are in those positions. Pay attention to the leaders in your organization who are highly admired and respected. And if you are a female, especially look at what the top females in your organization are doing—how they act, speak, and dress.

At Office Dynamics, we have been setting the standards for the administrative profession since 1990. We have been the visionaries and leaders in the industry. That is why so many Fortune 500 organizations bring us into their companies to train their assistants. They know our bar is very high and we challenge assistants to reach for the stars.

The big secret here is: don't always follow the crowd because they can be going in the wrong direction.

## WHAT NOW?

As a result of reading this chapter, what action steps are you going to take in the next 30 days to move in the right direction?

1. _____

_____

2. _____

_____

3. _____

_____

## WHAT OTHER THOUGHTS COME TO MIND?

*Always take the high road –*
*It is the one less traveled.*

# CHAPTER
# 15

# CREATE CONNECTIONS AND LONG-LASTING RELATIONSHIPS

**I BELIEVE PEOPLE ARE** our most important resource in the workplace. When I think back to my 20 years in the administrative profession, there is no way I could have accomplished what I did and completed my daily projects without the help of others. I needed people from various departments to help me. I relied on administrative peers to assist me during crunch times and teach me shortcuts. At one place where I worked, I needed the cafeteria staff to help give me my executive's lunch right away because he was heading off to an important meeting. I relied on couriers, town car drivers, florists, caterers, bankers, and the company pilot.

Building connections has certainly benefitted me and will do the same for you. When you genuinely get to know people and are accepting of them, they will help you in ways you cannot imagine. I'm not saying this will happen with every person you meet but overall, in time, it will help.

For decades, we have used the word networking. As of January 2018, I decided to change my language. Instead of saying networking, I started using connecting. It has an entirely different feeling and it truly identifies what we should be doing. We should be building connections (and sometimes deep connections) with people. We should be interested in others and their agenda.

## Worth Repeating: What's Holding You Back?

(Published in 2012) This is an excerpt from my book *Who Took My Pen … Again?* written along with Jasmine Freeman and Nancy Fraze and definitely worth repeating here.

You are someone others should meet. You are valuable and you have something to contribute. You could make a tremendous difference just by being friendly and meeting new people.

Why? At its very base, business is about connecting people. As you learn and become more comfortable connecting to people and then connecting people you know together, you will become a strategic networker. And that can easily translate into sales, knowledge, and opportunity.

The biggest obstacle to networking is insecurity. Too many people do not stretch themselves beyond their tiny comfort zones. These people prize safety and sameness. At meetings, they always sit with the same co-worker. They carpool to offsite meetings with that same person. They do not carry business cards. They arrive at meetings just on time, take a seat, and speak to no one. They cling to what is safe and comfortable and miss opportunities to make new friends, find jobs, and learn information that could help them.

It really boils down to this: You are worth meeting. You are worth knowing. You have something vital to share that no one else can: your perspective. If you withhold that from the world, it will be a smaller, sadder place. You belong to the world, so be willing to share yourself by becoming a good network aficionado.

## How to Build Connections

- Start by saying "hello." I can't tell you the number of people I pass who never say hello.

- Smile. Do you know how many people don't smile? A smile helps others smile. Your smile can open the door to the other person talking to you. I do this all the time. No, I'm not crazy. I smile when I order food. I smile at people when I walk on an airplane or through an airport. I smile at people as I walk through big corporate office hallways. It's amazing how others respond to a smile.

- A great way to start a conversation is to ask people about themselves. Everyone loves to talk about themselves or their life or their job. You can simply ask, "How is your day going?" Or, "What time do you get off your shift?"

- Sincerely compliment a person. We all appreciate a good compliment. You can say, "That color really looks great on you." Or tell a coworker, "I liked how you handled that situation." Or, "I admire the confidence you demonstrated in that meeting." Do you see that it is not hard? Just look for what people do well.

- Write notes or a letter. We can't always build connections face-to-face. For instance, maybe you met someone interesting at a conference or business meeting. Then you both go your own way—maybe you even live in different states or countries. You can keep your connection alive if you want to. Or there may be times when you never meet the person in person but you have read about them in an article or a press release. You can still write them a note card or letter and tell them what you think about their work, ideas, or causes.

**Introduce yourself.** Wende Morrow is an excellent example. Wende attended our Annual Conference for Administrative Excellence in Las Vegas in 2016. It was the first time she attended. Although Wende lived and worked in Las Vegas for years, and I have been in Las Vegas since 2000, she did not know of Office Dynamics until several months before our conference. We had 450 at our event that year.

In the midst of all those attendees, Wende purposely came to me and introduced herself. She talked about her passion for the profession and she was over-the-top excited to know that someone like me and Office Dynamics existed. Wende did not stop our connection there. She wrote Jasmine Freeman (former Office Dynamics employee) after the conference and copied me. Wende went on and on about how much she learned at our event and how she wanted to help in the future in any way possible. She would do it for free. Wende just wanted to a part of our cause.

Over the past few years, Wende has written me numerous times with brilliant ideas. She is an amazing writer and can paint a beautiful picture of what she is thinking. We have gone out to dinner and Wende has been a resource for me. She has recommended great books for me to read and even has sent me website links to informative blogs. As you can see, Wende truly stands out in my mind.

**A modern-day way of connecting is attending Facebook Live events.** Since February 2018, I have been hosting Facebook Friday. This is a vehicle I use to inspire people to end their week on a good note and provide a few quick tips. Several people have been able to jump on during the live event and post comments. I see the names come up and read the comments. Sometimes I respond. Almost every Friday there is a lady, Jordana, who is on. Jordana has also been attending several of my live e-courses this year. I now feel connected to Jordana. She contributes great ideas in the live e-courses and on Facebook Live. So of course, I want to get to know her. I admire her. And now Jordana is going to attend our Annual Conference for Administrative Excellence this fall in Las Vegas. I will personally meet her. And who knows where the future will take our relationship.

## I Want to Be Very Clear

Texting and emailing is not connecting. True connections are built by creating human moments ... sitting face-to-face, talking with each other, listening to each other, or getting a cup of coffee together. You have to genuinely care about the other person. When having human moments, be totally focused on the other person. Do not be glancing at your phone. Block out other distractions. Let the person you are with know that he or she is the most important thing at that moment!

## WHAT NOW?

As a result of reading this chapter, what action steps are you going to take in the next 30 days to move in the right direction?

1. _____

   _____

2. _____

   _____

3. _____

   _____


## WHAT OTHER THOUGHTS COME TO MIND?

_____

_____

_____

# CHAPTER
# 16

# DON'T
# LET ANYONE
# COLOR YOUR
# VISION

**AT 24, I LEARNED** to never let anyone at work color my vision of my boss or others in the workplace. I was working at an association headquarter's office in a suburb of Cleveland, Ohio. It wasn't exactly my ideal job but it was a good job. I worked for the head of the association. He was a nice elderly gentlemen. (Remember, I was only 24 so he seemed elderly to me.) I did some traveling in that job during the time I was employed. We held several conferences or mini-retreats for our members. And because I worked with the CEO and was quite involved in the planning, I traveled to each event. It was great fun and we traveled to some beautiful resorts.

There was another woman in the office who had worked there for many years. She also was young. Most often when we talked, she was negative. She would make negative comments about the association and my boss. (We said "boss" in those days.) Her comments finally got to me and I quit without having another job already lined up. I was married at the time. I remember sitting at home the first week after quitting my job, thinking, *What did I just do? I have no job and I actually liked the job I had*. After about a week, I called my old employer to see if I could return to work but was told no.

I learned at a very young age to never let anyone color my vision about a person, situation, or organization and you should also take heed. You should form your own views and opinions of people.

When co-workers talk about another co-worker, don't engage in the conversation. Stay neutral, or if you know that co-worker has some positive traits, stick up for him. Your co-worker may have had his own bad experience with that person or know what else has gone on behind the scenes.

Sometimes people are jealous! Yes, another assistant may be jealous of your position or your relationship with your executive.

Or could be upset because you got the job she wanted. It has happened many times.

Beware of jaundiced attitudes because they can be contagious. This is one of my biggest secrets. Since that age of 24, I have carried an invisible bubble around with me. This invisible bubble helps me let negative comments and attitudes bounce away from me. While I hear people's words, I try to not take them in. I'm not saying I never take them in. It's just that the majority of the time they bounce away from me. I also find if I keep my mind on my goals and dreams, I have less time to absorb negativity.

## WHAT NOW?

As a result of reading this chapter, what action steps are you going to take in the next 30 days to move in the right direction?

1. _____

_____

2. _____

_____

3. _____

_____

## WHAT OTHER THOUGHTS COME TO MIND?

_____

_____

_____

# CHAPTER
# 17

# BE THE CHANGE
# YOU WANT
# TO SEE

**YOU HAVE THE ABILITY** to create the kind of workplace you want to see. You are not at the mercy of top management. It is easy for employees to complain about what they don't like in their workplace or with their manager. It really is up to every individual to make their workplace a better place—to create an environment where people can prosper and be fulfilled.

Some examples are:

- If you want others to be open with you, then you need to be open with them first.

- Maybe you wish people would be more lighthearted when times are stressful. I am good friends with a woman who was the Chief Executive Assistant to a CEO of a major corporation. I'll never forget her telling me that when things got so intense at work, she ran over to a tree in the office that shed some leaves and jumped in them.

- One day several years ago, I had been very focused on my work in our office. At that time I had two employees, Jasmine and Michele. They were in their early 30s and liked to have fun with me. They had put on these funny hats and waited until I noticed them. I was so intense on my work, I walked right past them without noticing. They started laughing and that helped me relax. I'm not saying wear funny hats at work but be creative.

- Another example at the Office Dynamics office was a few years back when we were all on a wellness kick. We challenged each other during the day with various contests such as who could drink the most glasses of water that day. We had worksheets where we starred an item that demonstrated wellness that day. Do you see we created the environment we desired?

It's not that hard. It just takes commitment and a desire for things to be better. Yes, it takes some creativity and maybe a little work. It is worth it in the long run.

I can honestly tell you one of the reasons I was a highly-valued assistant is because I created and contributed to a good work environment. If we needed more polish and professionalism in our area, I demonstrated it. If we needed to improve our physical office environment, I pushed for new partitions or new artwork in our department.

Of course, to be able to do this you have to pay attention to the current state of your environment. Then picture how things could be better. Maybe your organization is going through some tough changes and employees need a boost with morale. What could you do to help that?

When you help create what you expect to see in the workplace, you are viewed as a leader and you gain a great deal of satisfaction and respect.

## WHAT NOW?

As a result of reading this chapter, what action steps are you going to take in the next 30 days to move in the right direction?

1. _____

_____

2. _____

_____

3. _____

_____

## WHAT OTHER THOUGHTS COME TO MIND?

_____

_____

_____

# CHAPTER
# 18

# EXCEL
# AT THE
# FUNDAMENTALS

**I KNOW MANY SEASONED** executive assistants who think they do not need to focus on or pay attention to their basic skills, what are also known as the fundamentals. In other words, they feel they have been managing calendars or planning meetings forever so why pay attention. This is not smart.

Since 1990, I have been teaching assistants to pay attention to the fundamentals such as meeting planning, travel planning, calendar maintenance, organizational skills, follow-up systems, time management, and communications. Every career has certain core fundamental skills. They are the foundation on which everything else is built. I have been a professional speaker since 1990. I never take for granted the basic 'platform' skills I learned in the early days as a speaker. I pay as much attention as ever and have meticulously polished those basics. That is why I am in high demand today.

You must do the same. Don't ever rest on your laurels. First of all, the world is moving at a much faster pace today so you have to be more organized, manage your projects better, take control of calendars, and cross every 't' and dot every 'i' when it comes to travel planning. Executives' expectations are high today and these are the key areas they want their assistants to excel in and then additionally want their assistants to develop advanced competencies.

My best-selling book *Inner Circle Assistant* focuses on the 12 core competency areas for assistants. They include:

- Appointment Coordination

- Manager Support

- Managing Office Technology

- Meeting Preparation and Coordination

- Office Communication

- Problem Solving

- Professional Behavior and Image

- Professional Development

- Supporting Multiple Managers

- Task and Project Management

- Time Management

If you have not read this book yet, I highly recommend you do so as I map out the strategies for excelling in these key areas.

At Office Dynamics, we are consistently surveying executives, managers, CEOs, human resources professionals, and organization development professionals on what skills, attitudes, and behaviors they look for in an assistant. Do you know what? The fundamentals always rise to the top. After that list, I see advanced competencies such as negotiation or persuasion skills. Over and over, time and again, there is proof that your fundamentals are critical to being successful in the administrative profession.

Also, when we conduct activities in our training classes with assistants and ask them what skills, attitudes, and behaviors are important for an assistant, 90 percent of the time they also list the fundamentals.

I highly encourage you to become a rock star at the fundamentals. There are always new ways of doing things and you can always streamline or fine tune your current processes. Think about how you can wow people in each of the areas I listed above.

## WHAT NOW?

As a result of reading this chapter, what action steps are you
going to take in the next 30 days to move in the right direction?

1. _____

   _____

2. _____

   _____

3. _____

   _____

## WHAT OTHER THOUGHTS COME TO MIND?

_____

_____

_____

# CHAPTER
# 19

# CHOOSE A
# POSITIVE
# ATTITUDE

**I HAVE BEEN SPEAKING** on attitude since **1990**. What I said in **1990** still holds true today. You have a choice when it comes to your attitude. You are not a victim of your circumstances. It is not what others do or say that matters; it's what you choose to do with what you have and choose how you want to respond.

Regardless of our individual circumstances, we all have one thing in common—we choose our attitude. That is great news because it means we can *change* it any time. If we feel the urge to get upset at someone, we can say to ourselves, "That's not going to help the situation any. I am going to stop, think, and then speak."

Our attitudes are delicate and fragile. If we do not take care of them, we are sure to feel the effects—everything from the quality of our work degrading to fading relationships. Did you know that your attitude also affects your health and even longevity?

> "Stress can ravage the body, unless the mind says no. A positive outlook can reduce the impact of stress on health." *(USA Today)*

> "Take this to heart: Happy people live longer than dour fuddy-duddies." *(USA Today)*

> "Optimists keep smiling. A study published by Mayo Clinic found that people who have optimistic outlooks live longer and healthier lives than their pessimistic counterparts." *(mayohealth.org)*

> "The power of positive thinking. Decades of research by Gallup has suggested that increasing positive emotions can expand a person's lifespan by as much as ten years." *(Real Simple)*

The challenge people face with attitude is they read books, listen to podcasts, watch Facebook videos, or hear motivational speakers on the subject but have a difficult time truly implementing it. That is because motivation is an inside job. It isn't something that happens to us; we have to create it. So, what can you do?

## Combat negativity

Listen to what you're saying to yourself. Instead of saying, "Nothing seems to be going right today," mentally rephrase it to, "Wow, I'm really being challenged today to think creatively." You are in control of your own thinking. You can change that old record and stop feeling like a victim. You can get support from family and friends, but you ultimately must take responsibility for your own attitude. Your sister may tell you that you look happy in the company photograph but if you tell yourself … *'happy' helps her avoid telling me that I gained weight,* you sabotage a compliment. Don't.

## Set goals and make a specific plan for your career

When you measure progress you feel in control. If your company offers continuing education opportunities, for example, and you complete two out of four successfully, 'notify' yourself that you're half way through the program. The *proverbial glass* is half-full and not half-empty. Most importantly, this is a solid achievement—one that is easily measured so you can hardly argue the point.

## Don't belittle your job or employer

Work provides you with a purpose, challenges you, puts food on your table, enables growth, and stimulates your thinking. Look at work as a gift. Be happy you have a job. It may not be ideal, but let's be realistic, no job is ideal. If you aren't feeling energy from your work, maybe it's because you aren't putting creative, positive energy into it.

## Develop a strong and diverse support system at work

It's fun and comfortable to be with people who are just like us. However, it is equally important to develop strong relationships with people who aren't just like us, especially in an era when team-work is critical to the success of a company. Push yourself out of your comfort zone. Start meeting people who are unique both in position and personality. Develop cross-functional relationships.

## Make the Right Choice

Life will always throw challenges at you. There will always be a 'Nancy Negative' or 'Don Dragon' trying to upset your attitude. You can make the decision every morning that you will face whatever comes your way with poise and tact.

And there's more ...

- Take control of your life and your actions.

- Make time for introspection.

- Develop a high tolerance for change.

- Focus on today and do the best you can in each moment.

- When you can't control the external climate, control the internal climate.

- De-clutter your life. Maybe there is too much going on.

I want to share with you my favorite quote. It says it all! You may want to post this at your desk.

## ATTITUDE by Charles Swindoll

*"The longer I live, the more I realize the impact of attitude on life. Attitude, to me, is more important than facts. It is more important than the past, than education, than money, than circumstances, than failures, than success, than what other people think or say or do.*

*It is more important than appearance, giftedness or skill. It will make or break a company ... a church ... a home. The remarkable thing is we have a choice every day regarding the attitude we will embrace for that day.*

*We cannot change our past ... we cannot change the fact that people will act in a certain way. We cannot change the inevitable. The only thing we can do is play on the one string we have, and that is our attitude.*

*I am convinced that life is 10 percent what happens to me and 90 percent how I react to it. And so it is with you – we are in charge of our attitudes."*

**WHAT NOW?**

As a result of reading this chapter, what action steps are you going to take in the next 30 days to move in the right direction?

1. _____

   _____

2. _____

   _____

3. _____

   _____

**WHAT OTHER THOUGHTS COME TO MIND?**

_____

_____

_____

# CHAPTER
# 20

# POSITION YOURSELF FOR THE FUTURE

IN MY WORLD CLASS ASSISTANT Certification and Designation course, I have been teaching assistants to be future-focused. It is so easy to focus on the daily 'to do' activities and not purposely stop and think about what is on the horizon six months, nine months, or even twelve months from today.

When I refer to being future-focused in this chapter, I am not talking about the future of your career. I am talking about:

- What is coming up on your leader's calendar?

- What new projects will need to be implemented to keep your organization competitive?

- How do you become more valuable to your executive by planning the next step and the three steps that follow?

## Why is it important?

- To stay on the cutting edge

- Decreases stress and pressure

- Helps you avoid 'fires'

- Avoids conflicting schedules

- Builds a sustainable infrastructure

- Blocks potential problems

- Provides some type of direction

- Allows for strategic business planning

## What can you look for?

The kinds of things you can and should look for:

- Budget changes

- The next big thing

- Social and economic trends

- Financial climate

- Procedures that will change and need to be implemented

- Leadership changes

- Threats

- Corporate vision

- Regulatory items (depending on your industry)

- Opportunities to get details

## How do you look to the future?

I'm sure this question is crossing your mind. How do you look to the future when the future has not yet happened? Well, I have answers for you.

- You can anticipate the future by paying attention to the present. If you really listen and pay attention to what is going on in your area or company, you can often predict future events.

- Look at the past. The past can give clues to trends that have occurred. Looking at the past can tell us what to do more of or what to do less of. For example, every year after we host our Annual Conference for Administrative Excellence, our team holds a debrief meeting. We go over every hour of our event, what happened, what worked well, and what did not work well. What hiccups occurred that we never could have anticipated. Often this information gives direction to what we do the at the following year's conference.

- Ask, "How can this go wrong?" Wow, that is a powerful question. This is an especially great question when considering new processes or ways of doing things. Or maybe hosting an event for the first time.

- Gauge your competition. While you may not feel this is your responsibility as an employee, you should still do this. You should pay attention to what is going on in the news that could affect your industry, which ultimately can affect you.

- Social media. Of course, you have to be selective as everything that goes out on social media is not true or accurate.

- Read! Read! Read! Open your mind to topics that are business related. It's really important to have some level of general knowledge.

- Connect with others. As you move through your day, listen to coworkers, managers, and people in other areas of the business.

- Look at and talk with the younger generation. I have been fortunate over the years to work closely with some younger people in our company. They were and are great at keeping me 'hip.' I pay attention to the terminology they use and they are a great resource when it comes to technology.

## CAUTION:

To be able to look to the future, you need to stop at least once throughout your day. Purposely make the time to look on the horizon. This takes discipline. It will not be easy at first, unless you are like me where my head is often in the future. Most CEOs, executives, and business owners are naturally blessed with this ability. That is why they are leading an organization. They have the ability to see possibilities, to see what could be, to look months and even years ahead. I promise you that if you grasp this skill, you will go far, be less stressed, be more proactive, and be way ahead of others around you who will not make time for this.

## WHAT NOW?

As a result of reading this chapter, what action steps are you going to take in the next 30 days to move in the right direction?

1. _____

   _____

2. _____

   _____

3. _____

   _____

## WHAT OTHER THOUGHTS COME TO MIND?

_____

_____

_____

# CHAPTER 21

# LOOK AT YOUR WORK WITH A QUESTION MARK

**THIS IS ALSO ONE** of my greatest and favorite secrets to success. A question mark means there is more to come. A period means stop, the end, this is it; there is no more or better. If I had lived by a period since I started my business, we would not be where we are today. If I had not planted hundreds of question marks in my mind over 27 years, my flagship training program, the Star Achievement Series, would not be in such high demand by large corporations like it is today.

The Star Achievement Series® is a perfect example. When I started writing this course in 1990 as I launched my business, there were only four full days of training. Each day we focused on different topics, but it was not called a series. It was just Star Achievement. The people who attended my classes in those early days loved the program so much, they asked if there was more. I said, "No, but I can write another set of four full-day workshops." That is when I structured Star Achievement into a Level I and a Level II. After a few years of teaching those two levels, attendees wanted more. They ate it up and did not want to stop so eventually I wrote a Level III.

An important part of this story is that over 28 years I had thoroughly revised that course 16 times! I was never satisfied with the first version or second or even the tenth. I kept asking myself:

- How can I make this better?

- How can I make this section more interesting?

- How can I present this information in a fun way?

- What other content do I need to make this meatier for attendees?

The questions went on and on. As good as Star Achievement is today, I know I will make updates in the future.

Now let's apply this to our daily activities. As I go through my day and my work, I ask myself:

- How could this be done faster?

- How can I streamline this process?

- How could I have handled that situation better?

- In what ways can I make this less stressful?

- Who can I involve to help me with this?

The subconscious is fascinating. You put questions in your subconscious and it looks for answers. You will not always get the answers right away. My answers have come to me while I was putting on makeup, in the supermarket, driving my car, and even in church. I will see something or hear someone say something that triggers an answer for my situation.

I just experienced this a few days ago. While we were focused on our 2018 Annual Conference for Administrative Excellence, I was already thinking about 2019. Every year, I select a theme for our event. That is what makes our conference an event of distinction. Important to note as well is that in 2018, we were hosting our 25th Annual Conference for Administrative Excellence and we were going all out (as usual). But I wondered, "How will we top this in 2019? What will we do?"

While I was walking through the Orlando airport about a month ago, I had some time to kill so I was looking for a new book to read. I stumbled upon a book called, *Successful Women Speak Differently*. Since a majority of assistants are female, I thought I could glean some new, good information to share with them as well as get new insights for myself.

I sat down with the book and started reading it. Within about an hour, I instantly thought of the theme for our 2019 conference. Voila! I was thrilled. This happens to me all the time. This has proven to be one of my greatest secrets and now you know my secret.

Look at work and your life with a question mark. You will be amazed at the answers and creative ideas that will come your way.

## WHAT NOW?

As a result of reading this chapter, what action steps are you going to take in the next 30 days to move in the right direction?

1. *I got this, I often do the some —picnic*

2. _____

3. _____

## WHAT OTHER THOUGHTS COME TO MIND?

_____

_____

_____

# CHAPTER
# 22

# BE A CAREER
# ENTREPRENEUR

**WHETHER OR NOT YOUR** company has formal annual performance evaluations, you should not sidestep assessing your performance and seeking to improve. You own your own career! Yes, you can 'settle' for just getting that paycheck (and I'm not suggesting getting a paycheck is a bad thing. We all have to manage our finances and need income.) But as a star-achieving assistant, you want more. You want growth, fresh expansion of your mind, and vision for your future.

Take your career in hand and manage it. Be a mentor or mentor others. If your company has a 360 or 180 review, participate. Ask your leaders for feedback and listen for the kernel of truth and reality. Read business books and see what you can implement. Then set a goal on your calendar to check in with yourself about how well you implemented and what happened.

The point is, you own your career and you should take growth and developing your potential very seriously. Put some time, effort, and motivation into it every year.

View yourself as a career entrepreneur. Career entrepreneurs manage their professions by outlining annual goals to ensure their success. Some of the benefits you derive from planning your goals are:

- Opening communication between you and your leader.

- Reminding your leader of your key accomplishments.

- Goal setting is based on your development plan.

- Providing tools to communicate long-term goals to your leader and co-workers.

- Putting you in charge of your future.

■   Staying fresh, being resilient, being considered a thought-leader.

Whether you are working your individual development plan or anticipating your performance review, you need to reflect on your accomplishments and plan for the upcoming year. It's also an excellent opportunity to update your resume with those achievements and new skills you've learned. Before you write your career action plan, you must first prepare for your review. Consider the following questions:

1.   What projects did you assist and teams did you serve on during the last twelve months? This is a good time to start keeping an activity log of projects, especially if you have a hard time remembering your key accomplishments from the previous year.

2.   What new skills did you learn as a result of taking on new responsibilities or attending professional development classes? Each year, inventory your skills to determine what needs to be added, developed, or maintained.

3.   How have you added value to your company? Eliminating unnecessary projects or steps in a process and streamlining tasks to increase profitability is necessary for all levels of the organization.

4.   How do *you* rate your performance? By writing your own performance review, you will be able to compare and intelligently discuss ratings with your leader.

## Seeking Input from Others

Another way to improve your performance is to solicit and encourage others to provide feedback. There are a variety of people you can ask for input such as other leaders, co-workers, internal, and external customers. Develop a form using the questions below to solicit feedback from others.

1.   What are my top skills? Ask each person to identify your strengths.

2.   In what areas would you like me to improve? Encourage others to be honest so that you can appropriately adjust your behavior.

3.   I'm interested in learning more about your responsibilities and your profession. Are there any projects that I can assist you with? They might be willing to give you a project so they can get involved in something different. This will also be a great opportunity for you to learn new skills.

4.   Do you have any additional suggestions to share with me? When receiving constructive criticism be open-minded and see it as an opportunity to improve yourself.

## Career Action Plan

It is the employees' responsibility to keep their skills current. Take the initiative to expand your responsibilities and look for opportunities to learn new skills, inside the company or from outside resources. Being active in your development plan will ensure your employability.

A career action plan helps you focus on your future growth and development. Development goals should answer three basic questions:

1.   What new skills do I need to develop? Determine what skill you need to learn, develop, or maintain.

2.   How will I develop them? State the desired method (classes, cross training, mentoring) for learning the new skill.

3.   When will I learn them? Set a target date for learning this new skill.

Progressive employees look for ways to accomplish their jobs that meet both the company's goals and their own goals. When you take care of your professional development, you are in control and can better manage your future. Set your goals high, be proactive, and you'll shine bright in your next review.

## Entrepreneurs Stay Motivated

When you run your own business, you must quickly learn to keep yourself motivated. This applies to you, too. If you have been an assistant for some time you can get bored, doing the same thing over and over. Setting up the same meetings and making travel plan can feel mundane after doing them often. However, any career professional can get bored after years of doing the same thing. Motivation is key and is especially challenging when you don't feel like doing anything! I'd like to share with you a piece I found several years ago from *Entrepreneur* Magazine.

## Find Your Purpose

"The first secret of motivation is that nobody else can motivate you. We can coerce or reward and get others to do things, but that's not motivation. Getting motivated requires lots of self-skills." – Dave Yoho

"Motivation is an inside job. You've got to do it yourself! Most of us operate at 10 percent of our potential because we are not fully motivated, and that's a crime. When you get on track with your purpose, you operate at 100 percent because you have fallen in love with your work." – Mark Victor Hansen

## Motivation Ebbs and Flows

Motivation isn't a perpetual-motion machine. It ebbs and flows even after we know our purpose, and that's natural. But there are surefire ways to kill motivation:

"Negative People-they are always out there. The antidote to negative people is to shut them out of your life and lock the door tight." —Mark Victor Hansen

"Fire Hoses-other people are potential problems, but often the bigger menace is ourselves. We're always ready with a dozen reasons why our ideas won't fly." —Bob Kriegel

"Fear — 97 percent of people live in fear, and that's why they are unmotivated. If you don't overcome your fears, they'll overcome you, leaving you unmotivated and immobilized." —Mark Victor Hansen

"Fear stifles our thinking and actions. It creates indecisiveness that results in stagnation. I have known talented people who procrastinate indefinitely rather than risk failure. Lost opportunities cause erosion of confidence, and the downward spiral begins." —Charles Stanley

## Sustaining Passion

Use Positives-a proven path to sustained motivation is to continually expose yourself to positive, upbeat people, events, and things (like books and tapes).

Don't ever stop learning and improving. When you continually strive for improvement, you always have something to look forward to.

Make time for quiet time. Are you willing to get contemplative, to look within? That's essential to staying motivated because it keeps us in touch with our purpose.

## Permanent Beta: Why Your Career is a Work in Progress

Here is another piece I absolutely love and share in our Star Achievement Series® course. It is by Reid Hoffman and Ben Casnocha, Special to CNN

*Editor's note: Co-founder and executive chairman of LinkedIn Reid Hoffman and writer Ben Casnocha are the authors of* The Start-up of You. *Here is a specially adapted excerpt from the book, about why applying a Silicon Valley mindset could help your career.*

CNN: Start-ups often keep the "beta test phase" label on their products for a time after the official launch to stress that the product is not finished so much as ready for the next batch of improvements.

Gmail, for example, launched in 2004 but only left official beta in 2009, after millions of people were already using it. Jeff Bezos, founder/CEO of Amazon, concludes every annual letter to shareholders by reminding readers, as he did in his first annual letter in 1997, that "It's still Day 1" of the internet and of Amazon.com.

For entrepreneurs, 'finished' is an F-word because they know that great companies are always evolving. 'Finished' ought to be an F-word for all of us. Because when it comes to our career, we are all works in progress. Each day presents an opportunity to learn more, do more, be more, and grow more, often in unexpected or unpredictable ways.

Keeping your career in permanent beta forces you to acknowledge that you have bugs, that there's new development to do on yourself; that you will need to adapt and evolve. It is a lifelong commitment to continuous personal and professional growth.

Entrepreneurs penetrate the fog of the unknown by testing their products and their hypotheses through trial and error. Any entrepreneur (and any expert on cognition/learning) will tell you that practical knowledge is best developed by doing, not just thinking or planning.

In the early days of LinkedIn, the plan was to have members invite their trusted connections by email—an invitation mechanism that would fuel membership growth. But it turned out that the best way to enable viral spread was to enable members to upload their address books and see who else was on the service already.

For careers you don't know what the best plan is until you try. Lunging at the first well-paid and/or high-status job you come upon may offer immediate gratification, but it won't get you any closer to building a meaningful career. Entrepreneurs deal with uncertainties, changes, and constraints head-on. They take stock of their assets, aspirations, and the market realities to develop a competitive advantage.

They craft flexible plans. They build a network of relationships throughout their industry that outlives their current venture. They aggressively seek and create breakout opportunities that involve focused risk, and actively manage that risk. They tap their network for the business intelligence to navigate tough challenges. And they do these things from the moment they hatch that nascent idea to every day after that—even as their companies go from being run out of a garage to occupying floors of office space.

Companies act small to retain an innovative edge no matter how large they grow. That is why Steve Jobs famously called Apple the "biggest start-up on the planet."

To succeed professionally in today's world, you need to adopt this same permanent beta mindset.

In the same way entrepreneurs are always improving and investing in their products, you need to always be improving and investing in yourself.

You need to stay young and agile. You need to draw up plans but be nimble enough to stray from those plans when appropriate. You must be persistent in fulfilling your vision, but also be ready to shift course based on the changing demands of the job market or economic landscape. You must be ever evolving.

And in the same way that entrepreneurs are always improving and investing in their products, you need to always be improving and investing in yourself.

Make a plan to develop skills and experiences that are broadly useful to potential other jobs. Writing skills, general management experience, technical and computer skills, people smarts, and international experience or language skills are examples of skills with what we call high option value—that is, they are transferable to a wide range of possible options.

Once you've figured out which transferable skills to invest in, make a concrete action plan you can stick to, whether by signing up for a course or conference, or simply by pledging to spend one hour each week teaching yourself something.

Begin on an experimental side project that you work on during some nights and weekends. Orient it around a skill or experience that is different but related to what you do now. Ideally, collaborate on this project with someone else in your network.

Do whatever it takes to keep yourself relevant. Because winning careers, like winning start-ups, are in permanent beta: always a work in progress. Keeping your career in 'permanent beta' means continuous growth.

---

**WHAT NOW?**

As a result of reading this chapter, what action steps are you going to take in the next 30 days to move in the right direction?

4. _____

_____

5. _____

_____

6. _____

_____

---

**WHAT OTHER THOUGHTS COME TO MIND?**

_____

_____

# CHAPTER
# 23

# WHO IS YOUR BOARD OF TRUSTEES?

**I WILL NEVER FORGET** the time a wise assistant I know, Sherry Viering, asked the class, "Who is on your Board of Trustees? Who do you surround yourself with? Who do you go to when you have challenges or questions? Who is giving you appropriate guidance?"

I have known Sherry Viering for years. She is a top-notch executive assistant. I have been fortunate to work with Sherry as she is the individual who has been coordinating onsite training for assistants at Nationwide Insurance. Every year, I go to Nationwide in Columbus, Ohio and teach our World Class Assistant Certification and Designation course. We usually hold one or two sessions a year with 20 – 25 participants each. Since I started doing this training with Sherry and Nationwide Insurance, we have had 140+ Nationwide assistants earn their CWCA designation (Certified World Class Assistant).

I pose Sherry's questions to you. What kinds of people do you surround yourself with at work? Who gives you guidance and honest feedback? Do you have a broad network of diverse individuals you can reach out to?

I belong to a group called Vistage in Las Vegas. Vistage is an international organization. Vistage is the world's leading business advisory and executive coaching organization designed exclusively for CEOs, business owners, and key executives.

In my group are 12 individuals, all with unique business backgrounds and experiences. We have female and male members. We meet every month for a full day (7:30am – 5:30pm), with very few breaks and short lunches. We cover an immense range of topics. We spend part of the day digging deep into members' issues. We get in the dirt and tell each other what we NEED to hear, not what we want to hear. Our goal is to help each other be successful and not act like victims of our circumstances.

Who are your friends at work and who are your advisors? They should portray the following:

- Tell you what you *need* to hear to be successful.

- Know when to have empathy.

- Tell you when you need to stop playing the victim.

- After you have complained to them about whatever is going on at work, they tell you, "I understand how you can feel that way. Now go back out there and get the job done."

- Provide interesting perspective.

- Offer suggestions.

- Be an excellent listener.

- Give open and honest feedback.

Over 40+ years' experience in the business world, I have carefully chosen who is on my Board of Trustees and with whom I personally surround myself. I do not have time for Debbie Downers or Ned Naysayers. I will not tolerate people who feel like a weight around my ankle. You have a choice as to whom you hang around with and you need to choose wisely.

**WHAT NOW?**

As a result of reading this chapter, what action steps are you going to take in the next 30 days to move in the right direction?

1. _____

   _____

2. _____

   _____

3. _____

   _____

**WHAT OTHER THOUGHTS COME TO MIND?**

_____

_____

# CHAPTER
# 24

# SLAY THE
# DRAGONS

'**FIGHTING OFFICE DRAGONS' IS** one of the most popular segments of our Star Achievement Series® training program for assistants. We talk about perceived dragons vs. real dragons, ineffective fighting tactics people use to slay the dragons and why they don't work, and then go into real-world strategies. I am sharing here the most important pieces for you to know.

Dragons were huge, dominating, fictitious creatures. Medieval writers had vivid imaginations for big, scary things. For many people, work is like a dragon. It can be overwhelming and certainly dominates well over half of our waking hours. Sometimes the people we work with can be pretty 'fiery' creatures to deal with, too. In dragon fighting, the important thing to remember is that it's a matter of the mind. Take care of your attitude today … it is your primary weapon against office dragons!

There are many dragon species at work. Three of the most common perceived species are leaders, co-workers, and self. Yes, you can be a dragon to yourself. Let's look at each one of these.

## Leaders

When I ask assistants what are some things managers do that make them appear to be dragons, these are the typical responses I hear. See if you can relate to any of them.

Leaders can appear to be dragons when they:

- don't communicate on the employee's level

- give poor direction

- don't provide necessary information

- show favoritism

- don't follow through on what they say

- set unrealistic expectations

- procrastinate

- don't resolve conflicts

- are inflexible

There really are some dragon leaders, but most of the time, leaders are not dragons. They just appear to be that way to employees. People in management positions usually have good reasons for taking certain actions and for making the decisions they make.

Here are some questions to consider when you feel your leader or other managers are portraying dragon-like behaviors.

## What school did this dragon go to?

*Consider*

There are many management styles. Some leaders believe the best way to get people to do what they want is through intimidation and fear. Other leaders believe in empowering employees and motivating them through positive feedback. Which school of thought do your leaders follow?

*Consider*

Who were their teachers? The people your leaders worked for during their careers had an impact on them, positive or negative. Look at your leader as individuals. Consider such things as their background, who they worked for, and what kind of training they received, if any.

*Consider*

They are individuals with unique backgrounds and experiences. Each was raised in a different environment with various circumstances. What we experience as we grow up and live in a household with parents or family influences who we are as we get older, unless we actively choose to change our beliefs.

## What is your dragon's communication style preference?

Employees who think their leaders don't communicate clearly or provide enough information may not be taking a close look at their leader's communications style. We all have our own way of taking in information and sending it out.

Get to know your leader's style of communication. Does she like information short and to the point? Does she need facts and detail? Once you identify your leader's style, you can communicate in the way that will be most effective. Your leader will be more open to input if it's presented in a format she likes. By not tapping into your leader's style, you reduce openness to your information or idea.

Sometimes leaders are just too busy and don't realize they aren't communicating something of importance to their employees. They have major projects on their minds, meetings to attend, phone calls to make, and employee problems to handle. You can improve the communication process by asking questions.

Other times employees just aren't supposed to know everything that is going on. Leaders use their best judgment as to when to share information with staff.

## Do leaders really have unrealistic expectations?

Today everything moves at hypersonic speed. No matter how fast it is, we want it to go faster! Yet with the drive for speed is an equal necessity for quality. Companies can't afford to sacrifice quality or re-work. Companies strive to have skilled, knowledgeable employees with the best products and services. They need employees who continually seek improvement and higher quality. Your company shouldn't have to tell you to do this; you need to embrace a philosophy of continuous improvement in your work.

It is natural for a leader to expect the best of people. It can be seen as a compliment. The leader is saying, "I believe you can do great things. I believe in your skills and abilities. I believe in you." Is that so bad?

An interesting facet of life in the fast lane is that because of that speed, no one stops often or long to think long and hard about what they are asking you to do really means or entails fully. Specifics and details may be unknown to your leader, or even glossed over, unintentionally.

Leaders don't always know every little detail a request might create or moment by moment, what your job entails. They don't see that their request causes a domino-like effect, a cascade of additional workflow.

Leaders see your position from their perspective and you see their position from your perspective. Neither of you realize how long it may take to perform a particular task or the small army of people who may be needed. And leaders may not recognize the demands put on you by others in activities that swirl around your desk.

## Co-workers

Here are the typical answers I hear from workshop participants about co-workers and how they can appear to be dragons.

- gossip

- convey a bad mood at the office

- bring personal problems to the office

- don't perform their part of a job

- aren't a team player

- don't share necessary information

- complain

- have a 'that's not my job' attitude

Soon you will read my strategies for dealing with the dragons. The important piece to remember here is to make sure you are not being a co-worker dragon. Maybe you aren't always a team player or sometimes you bring your personal problems to the office. Maybe without realizing it, you convey a bad attitude.

## Yourself

Yes, you can be a dragon to yourself whenever you do any of the following:

- don't focus on the job

- let others damage your attitude

- lack assertiveness

- don't see your own potential

- try to please everyone

- fall into dragon habits

- lack confidence

- take criticism personally

You can do more harm to yourself with negative thinking than any outside dragon. It is your thought process and attitude that controls your internal dragon. You have the power at any time to tame your dragon and put out the fire of any dragon-like qualities.

## Weapons to Win

There is one tactic that will truly slay dragons. Face them! Dragons won't go away unless you learn to face them in a positive fashion. Here are suggestions on how to face dragons professionally. Remember, this includes when you are a dragon to yourself.

## Act ... Don't React

Reaction cycles never end. Only when you decide to think and act independently will you progress toward your goal. Reacting is responding to your immediate feeling. It puts you at the mercy of the dragon.

Acting is proactive. It's thinking through what is happening and taking positive steps. It seeks a win/win, not a win/lose. This makes you feel good about what could be a negative situation. You probably will respond differently to a situation if you act rather than react.

## Stop the Mindreading!

Face it, we all move so fast that we seldom take initiative to clarify things with others. Instead, we ponder a scenario, rolling it over and over in our minds. We 'determine,' i.e., mind read, what that person was thinking/motivated by/perceiving, without simply asking them to clarify.

## Educate the Dragon

Some dragons don't even know they are dragons. Think about how, when, and where you can approach the dragon to talk about his or her behaviors. Try to help the dragon see the negative impact of these behaviors and provide positive techniques the dragon can use to combat them.

## Confront the Dragon

There are certain dragon species you need to confront head on. I had to do this in my 20s when I was a secretary. My situation turned out to my benefit because I followed the steps below. You have to be careful how and when you confront the dragon and what words you use. You want the person to know you are serious and want the dragon-like behaviors to stop.

Keep in mind the following:

1.  Make sure you have all the facts about the situation.

2.  Have a plan before confronting the dragon face to face. Decide when and where you will talk to the dragon, how you will do this, and what you will say.

3.  Use non-threatening language. You don't want to lower your standards and be like the dragon. You can make your point by selecting appropriate words and being firm.

4.  Let the dragon know your speech, body language, and facial expression that you mean business.

5.  Make eye contact with the dragon.

6.   State your expectations for future behavior.

7.   If it happens again, confront the dragon again.

## Focus on Self-Change vs. Changing Others

A good first step is communicating with the dragon. Informing someone and offering suggestions can sometimes be helpful, because people don't always see their negative attitude or behavior. In the final analysis, however, every adult does as he or she chooses. When you can't change a situation or a person's behavior, look at changing your view about this person. You can still control your attitude.

## Take Independent Steps Toward Your Goals

Determine what your goals are and write them down. List the one thing you can do toward achieving those goals each day. Doing this combines the winning strategies of independent action and self-change. Setting and achieving goals gives you a sense of accomplishment. This is a positive feeling. When you feel good about who you are and what you do, it naturally flows over to others.

## Enjoy What You Are Doing

If you feel bored, stagnant, or overwhelmed, maybe you are not putting enough positive energy into your work. Decide to look for the good in your job and how to make it more fun. Be creative and you will have more energy. Find challenge and enjoyment in your work by doing it differently, finding a better or easier way, doing it to the best of your ability, and with pride. If you've been in your position for a long time, you might be feeling unchallenged. You can change that in a moment.

## Take Control

Maybe you cannot control how much work or what kind of work is given to you, but you can establish the priorities, the manner or format, and how you organize it. You can control how you accept responsibility. Can you rise to the challenge when given certain tasks or do you complain? Being organized, knowledgeable, and positive about work and people gives you a sense of control.

## Make Friends

You spend more time with co-workers than you do with your family or friends. People at work must become allies instead of dragons. The work relationship requires respect, honesty, confidentiality, appreciation, communication, and energy.

Almost every organization has a dragon floating around. Is there a dragon you can help? Are there people at work you can be-friend? Remember, even dragons need a friend or two.

# Beware of the Black Hole

By Karla Weaver, Star Achievement Series® Graduate

"I participated in a Star Achievement class where we discussed the different varieties of stars in the universe: pulsating stars, twin stars, and exploding stars. During the small group discussion, I couldn't help but think about another type of star—the black hole.

In simple terms, a black hole is a star that is collapsing in on itself. Around this region of space is a boundary or 'point of no return,' the point at which the gravitational pull becomes so great that nothing can escape, not even light.

Have you encountered someone who is a 'black hole' in your personal or professional life? If you get too close, you get pulled into a negative sphere. And once you're there, it can take a tremendous amount of effort to extricate yourself.

Star performers know that we have to employ healthy boundaries to keep ourselves from being sucked into pessimism and darkness. As Joan Burge often says, "Attitude is a choice." We can choose to deal tactfully with the black holes in our lives to keep our attitudes positive, or we can choose to allow them to suck us into negativity. Attitude is a choice. Choose well.

## WHAT NOW?

As a result of reading this chapter, what action steps are you going to take in the next 30 days to move in the right direction?

8. _____

_____

9. _____

_____

10. _____

_____

## WHAT OTHER THOUGHTS COME TO MIND?

_____

_____

# CHAPTER
# 25

# IT'S SHOWTIME!

**WHETHER YOU DECIDE YOU** want to move up in your chosen field, move out of the profession, or stay where you are, a career portfolio will be a valuable asset for you. It's not enough to just 'tell' people what you do or to give them a resume. In today's competitive job market, where you might be competing against ten other top-notch assistants interviewing for one job, you must use tools that will give you the edge. Think of a career portfolio as a show-and-tell giving the potential employer a picture of your accomplishments, demonstration of your skills, and an impression that you are serious about your profession.

Why would it be beneficial to create a career portfolio?

- Shows you are proactive.

- You'd have a hard copy of your accomplishments; permanent history.

- Shows people what you are capable of doing.

- A tool to receive higher levels of recognition.

- Shows your creativity.

## When and where can you use it?

- During your performance review.

- When writing your professional development plan for the upcoming year and tracking accomplishments.

- Competing for an internal job.

- When a new boss comes on board and you want the boss to quickly gain an overview of your talents and experiences.

- Asking for additional responsibility.

- Outside work – if you are trying to obtain a leadership role.

- When being considered for committee work.

- External interviewing.

## What can you put in this portfolio? Many things but here are some suggestions:

- Professional photo of yourself (no larger than 4 x 6).

- Record of any outside work, volunteer, or committee work.

- Thank-you notes from customers or clients.

- Thank-you letters from other divisions or executives.

- Examples of your work: graphic work; spreadsheets (be careful not to divulge confidential company information).

- Past evaluations (not more than 3 years).

- Your mission statement and vision.

- Customer appreciation letters.

- Resume (have extra copies in the back pocket if you use a three-ring binder).

- Emphasize results and accomplishments vs. job duties!

## Packaging Your Portfolio (this says a lot about you right away!)

Be sure to place this information in a nice binder or casing. Many assistants have gone above and beyond by getting a leather portfolio embossed with their initials on it. You may feel more comfortable using a three-ring binder when you start the formation of your portfolio. Be creative. Remember the outside packaging also represents you and will send a message to the person viewing your portfolio. Think clean lines, professional-looking, and quality products. Also think about the font style and size you will use—again, keep it professional. Consider the details right down to the type and color of paper you will use. Sheet protectors will provide your portfolio protection from the hands that will be holding it as well as easy access to simply change out and update your information.

For ease of browsing, it is recommended that you tab your portfolio and name each section accordingly. This is another way to add your own personal touches to your portfolio. Some creative terms or tab names used have been:

- Employee Advocate

- Credentials

- Strategic Partner

- Visual Identification (photo)

- Career History

- Specified Training

Extras can include a Table of Contents, cover letter, an informational CD, or a link to the soft copy version of your career portfolio.

Remember, this is a tool to showcase your talents and open the conversation up with your leader or interviewer. Give them a chance to ask you questions—you don't need to put every single detail in the portfolio (think 'at a glance') as your reader will likely thumb through the pages. Avoid text-heavy pages.

Note: Do not leave this portfolio with the interviewer or others reviewing your portfolio. That is why you may wish to keep a copy of your career portfolio online.

Having a physical representation of your career portfolio is important because it shows an executive that you are serious about your career and you care enough to take the time to nurture this portfolio and showcase your work professionally. However, you won't want to make a new portfolio with each interview or chance the possibility of the reviewer losing or damaging it. Yet you do want to have a way to showcase your work to someone who wants to have more time to review your portfolio. The perfect way to 'leave' your information with someone is to keep a digital version of your career portfolio. Available online or in a PowerPoint as a soft copy.

## Keeping a Digital Career Portfolio

There are multiple ways of showcasing your work in a digital format. Here are just a few examples.

- Blog

  » Link directly to your work on the worldwide web.
  » Your own space, you aren't relying on another site owner.

- LinkedIn

  » Great space to house testimonials of your work.
  » Online resume.
  » Excellent search ability of your resume if you are looking but a necessary tool for all business professionals (searching or not).

- SlideShare or Prezi

  » PowerPoint style presentations
  » Work with other sites such as LinkedIn

Be careful using sites that don't belong to you when showcasing your information. If they change their terms of use or even shut down the site you could potentially lose your portfolio and all that hard work you put into it will have been for nothing.

Start simply with a PowerPoint presentation that you can link to testimonials featured on your LinkedIn profile (Recommendations and Endorsements). You can also hyperlink your reader directly to your written work (Blogs) and video work (YouTube) if applicable. The options are endless and it's all unique to your own skills and abilities. To house your slideshow online you can utilize such tools as SlideShare or Prezi. LinkedIn also works with such presentation sites to add your online portfolio directly into your online resume.

With all these tools comes a certain amount of maintenance. Keep a folder for portfolio updates in your follow-up and make updates to your preferred tools and hard copy version three to four times per year when you aren't currently on the market, and more frequent attention when you are searching for a job.

## WHAT NOW?

As a result of reading this chapter, what action steps are you going to take in the next 30 days to move in the right direction?

1. _____
   _____

2. _____
   _____

3. _____
   _____

## WHAT OTHER THOUGHTS COME TO MIND?

_____

_____

# CHAPTER
# 26

# SET HEALTHY
# BOUNDARIES

**THE ADMINISTRATIVE PROFESSION HAS** changed and so have those in the profession. While many assistants already are confident and express their views and opinions, tens of thousands of assistants still want to know how they can set healthy boundaries in the workplace without offending others or losing their job. So, you are not alone.

## What Happens If You Don't Set Healthy Boundaries?

- Work longer hours.

- Use personal time to sift through emails (exception—if that is part of your job).

- Take on more work than you should.

- Feel personally attacked.

- Stressed.

- Feel underappreciated.

- Are underutilized.

- People take advantage of your good nature.

- Sacrifice your needs for others (and resent the person later).

- You won't fulfill your potential.

Sheryl Sandberg, COO of Facebook and author of *Lean In* says, "We are a generation suffering greatly from an endless work schedule—we must set boundaries or we will crash at some point. I guarantee it." Sheryl is talking about setting personal boundaries in terms of turning off the technology and not be accessible every minute of the day to everyone. Setting boundaries goes way beyond technology.

## Why It Matters!

We all have needs to be met in the workplace so we can do our job and finish projects on time. We also have to make sure people do not walk all over us. The benefits to us are:

- Feeling in control.

- Build confidence in your capabilities.

- Helps achieve our goals.

- Gain self-confidence.

- Improved communications.

- Create win-win situations.

- Expand your influence.

- Gain greater job satisfaction.

Setting boundaries requires a delicate balance of various skills. I've had years of practice—as an executive assistant for 20 years and female business owner for over 28 years. Yet I'm always working on setting boundaries because situations and people change.

> *We teach people by our actions, how we will and will not be treated; and how we think, feel, and behave. When someone violates our rights and we don't say anything, we teach them it's okay to dominate and manipulate us. We therefore create stress in our lives. The best time to assert yourself is early in the relationship.*
> **—JOAN BURGE**

Before I get into how to set boundaries, I'm going to start by explaining the differences between passive, aggressive, and assertive. Setting healthy boundaries is about being assertive.

Passive: A passive person *only* cares *about what others* think and making sure everyone else's needs are met. You might be thinking, *Isn't that a good thing?* No. Not when we sacrifice ourselves or what we need to get done for the sake of others. Passive people can become resentful or blow up later, which then becomes aggressiveness. Passive communication is when you bend over backwards not to hurt another person, beat around the bush, avoid honesty, avoid eye contact, apologize for your feelings, whine or complain.

Aggressive: Aggressive people *only care about themselves*; they don't care what they say or how they say it as long as they get what they want. Aggressive communication is when all you care about are your needs, doing whatever it takes to get what you want at the expense of others.

Assertive: Assertive people *care that their own needs* are met AND *care about others.* They think about how they will communicate in a caring way and still get what they need. Assertiveness is saying what you mean and asking for what you want in a clear, factual, and straightforward manner and without apology.

The 3 essential skills of assertiveness are: verbal, non-verbal (body language), and cognitive (our thought processes). If we are to succeed in being assertive, all 3 elements must be in place. This means avoiding being passive or aggressive in approach in order to deal with the situation constructively and not provoke a negative reaction in those we are dealing with.

## Attitude of Confidence

Assertiveness has to do with having an 'attitude of confidence.' It is an attitude of self-respect; it is an attitude of respecting other people's rights. It is an aura of confidence. When you are assertive, you not only ensure that your needs are met to get the job done, but you actually help others be more efficient and effective.

> Article by Heather Shuttleworth, "Top 10 Tips for Assertiveness."

> One of the biggest challenges for professionals today is being assertive. Assertiveness means being your own best advocate and ensuring you do not get taken advantage of. It requires a certain amount of courage to avoid passivity, as well as the tact to avoid aggression and serves as a happy middle ground between the two. Being assertive can be a useful skill in many different ways, but is particularly vital for setting and maintaining healthy boundaries; especially for women.

Ninety-seven percent of administrative professionals are female so this is a vital skill to develop.

Being assertive will not be easy for everyone. It is a skill you can learn and the more you do it, the more comfortable you become. This does not mean, though, that you will never feel intimated. Again, situations change and the people we interact with change.

The Little Voice: We all have a little voice inside our heads. Sometimes the voice is helpful and other times it is not. You have to ensure that your thoughts are supporting assertive behavior. This works best when participants are prepared to work together openly.

## In Person vs. E-mail or Text

The #1 priority when setting boundaries is to talk to the person, in person, face-to-face. If that is not absolutely possible, then #2 is to talk to the person on the telephone. My #3 choice would be Skype or Facetime. This could also be the #2 choice.

## 7 Steps to Being Assertive

1. Outwardly confront something instead of holding it in or stewing over it. Passive people hold things in. They keep their feelings buried and do not like confrontation. Therefore, they are walked over and stressed out. While you may want to take some time to think about the situation and how you want to respond, do not sit on it for days and weeks. In fact, the sooner you confront a situation or something someone said to you, the better. Just choose your words carefully.

2. State your opinions clearly. You are entitled to your opinion. We are not clones of each other. When communicating with others take time to be clear when expressing your opinions and especially do not say anything that would hurt another person's feelings.

3. Walk away at your choosing. Passive people walk away because they feel intimidated by a person or the situation. An assertive person walks away because it's just not worth more time or energy.

4. Be active, not reactive. Assertive people take action but they also stop and think before they take action. Again, they craft the message they want to deliver so the other person will be open to what they say.

5.   Establish deadlines. You can start this today! Many executive and administrative assistants will ask, "When do you need this?" Of course, the common answer is, "As soon as you can get it to me," or, "As soon as possible." Learn to ask people, "By when do you need this?" Get the people who assign you tasks or special projects to commit to the *latest* date by which they need something, not the soonest. This helps the person giving you the assignment set his own priorities and helps you prioritize your workload.

6.   Do not accept inappropriate behavior. If there is anything that does not feel right or appropriate to you in the workplace, you must tell the offending person the action or words are not acceptable to you. A very simple example for assistants is the person who always comes into the assistant's workspace and takes pencils or pens or whatever. If you don't like that, say something. That is a very simple example. My point is you do not have to accept behaviors that make you frustrated, stressed, or uncomfortable. My favorite saying is, "People will continue to treat you *as you allow* them to."

7.   Go to the source. People tend to complain to their friends or co-workers about someone at work who upset them or they don't like. That does not change the situation or how you feel—at least not permanently. When something arises with another person, you need to go directly to the source. Again, use positive communication skills. If you hear something via third party, make sure you have all your facts before going to the source.

## Risk Awareness

RECOGNIZE

When you dare to set boundaries, it's important to weigh the risk because you aren't guaranteed of the outcome. You have to be willing to take a chance, knowing things may not turn out like you hope. However, you have a better chance having your needs met through assertive action than by being passive or aggressive.

There is a higher risk level if you are setting boundaries with your executive than a peer. Your executive is still the executive and your boss. If you need to negotiate your work load with your executive, then talk to your executive.

Again, face to face communication.

MINIMIZE the risk involved so your message is received and your professional image remains intact.

## Weigh the Pros and Cons

If you are doubtful as to whether to assert yourself in a particular situation, you should weigh the pros and cons. CAUTION: It is not the number of pros vs. cons that is as important as the impact of each pro and con. You might have five pros on your list and only one con. But if the weight of the con is far greater than the weight of the pros, then don't take action.

## START WITH THE END IN MIND

Start with Expected Outcome ➡ Use Assertive Communication ➡ Experience Positive Results

Setting healthy boundaries is all about communication—verbal and non-verbal, plus being confident and caring. Here are some specific techniques:

- State exactly what you want to happen or exactly what you need.

- By when does this have to happen?

- Use "I" statements.

- Purposely use impact words, such as 'need' vs. 'would be nice if …'

- Speak clearly and with a confident tone.

- Write with confidence and be concise.

## WHAT NOW?

As a result of reading this chapter, what action steps are you going to take in the next 30 days to move in the right direction?

1. _____

_____

2. _____

_____

3. _____

_____

## WHAT OTHER THOUGHTS COME TO MIND?

_____

_____

# CHAPTER
# 27

# INTERPERSONAL
# SKILLS GIVE
# YOU THE EDGE

**OUTSTANDING ADMINISTRATIVE PROFESSIONALS NOT** only have excellent business skills but also excellent interpersonal skills. They realize that these skill sets are as important to their business success as appropriate excellence in the performance of any of their basic work duties. Daniel Goleman wrote the 'bible' on interpersonal skills in his book, *Emotional Intelligence – why it can matter more than IQ.* The Harvard Business Review hailed emotional intelligence (EI) as "a ground-breaking, paradigm-shattering idea," one of the most influential business ideas of the decade. Today, companies worldwide routinely look through the lens of EI in hiring, promoting, and developing their employees.

While many administrative office professionals have become technically proficient, they have not similarly focused on their people skills. If you think about your day, what do you do all day in some way, shape, or form? The answer: You interact with people! Even if you are sending an email, that message is going to be read and evaluated by a person. When you leave a voice message, a person is going to listen to it.

I have often seen administrative professionals overlooked for promotions or kept from top positions because of poor interpersonal skills. If you think interpersonal soft skills don't matter, you had better think again. You are exposed to a multitude of people inside and outside the organization. Your business and personal success will depend on your ability to handle situations and people with tact, poise, and discretion.

Whether you call them interpersonal skills or soft skills, they are necessary for business and relationship success. I have been teaching soft skills to all levels of administrative professionals in every industry since 1990. In fact, all the programs Office Dynamics International has written and taught are soft or interpersonal skills. Our research proves over and over that executives of all levels, from Human Resources manager to Training and Development professionals, put soft and interpersonal skills at the top of their list in what they look for in an administrative or executive assistant.

Administrative professionals themselves have identified soft skills being required to be successful in the profession. In our World Class Assistant™ certification course, the first question we ask attendees is "How would you describe a World Class Assistant? What words would you use to describe this person? What skills, behaviors, and attributes would this person possess?" 90 percent of the list the participants create is around interpersonal or soft skills.

Here is a very small portion of the answers we have received over the years. How would you rate yourself in each of these?

| Proactive | Organized | Professional |
|---|---|---|
| Team Player | Flexible | Approachable |
| Trustworthy | Respectful | Knowledgeable |
| Teachable | Intuitive | Diffuser |
| Excellent communicator | Future-focused | Positive |
| Works well with others | Educator | Open to new ideas |
| Takes initiative | Strategic partner | Cool under pressure |
| Good listener | Detail oriented | Perceptive |

Here are a few soft skills that most people do not consider yet should be part of a star assistant's repertoire:

- Builds consensus

- Takes risks

- Ability to change your mental outlook

- Overcomes intimidation in the workplace

- Leverages criticism

- Displays courage at work

- Stays motivated

- Encourages feedback from your leader on work performance

- Sets goals

- Can be flexible and adaptable

- Is solution-oriented

- Demonstrates leadership

- Builds peer synergy

- Anticipates problems

> *Your business and personal success will depend on your ability to handle situations and people with tact, poise, and discretion.*

As you can see, the expectations are huge. Your technical skills are critically important because those are the tools to help you get your job done. The question is, how good would you be at your job if all the technology was taken away? I'll use an analogy from my field of professional speaking. Awesome professional speakers don't need any technology. They rely on their own talents, speaking ability, communications, and being able to think on their feet. PowerPoint and other fun techy tools are used to enhance their work, not replace it.

It should be the same with you. Star assistants and world class assistants receive higher scores on their soft skills. In a world where everyone relies on technology but lack people skills, you will stand out when you develop your soft skills. So, what are some of those areas that you need to develop? Before I answer that I want to tell you that no matter how good you are today, there is always room for improvement. As someone who has been inspiring excellence in administrative professionals since 1990 through training and coaching, I can tell you there is always room to excel.

First, communication is probably the largest area that you should work on. This skill area is huge. There are many facets under communications. I could spend weeks teaching communication skills. I identified some areas to work on in the chart.

## Communication Areas of Development

| Assertive Communications | Listening skills (Listening is active; hearing is passive. They are not the same.) | Being aware of people's moods and adjust your communications accordingly | Understanding communication styles and know when to stretch into another person's style |
|---|---|---|---|
| Persuasion skills | Negotiation skills | Selling ideas up and down the organization | Communicating effectively with difficult people |
| Recognizing communication deterioration and knowing what to do and say | Building rapport | Body language and facial expression | Presentation skills |
| Knowing how to communicate with various generations | Knowing what to say when someone has criticized you or your work | Initiating purposeful communication with your executive | Cultivating business relationships through communication |
| Being adept at delivering difficult messages in a tactful manner | Having critical conversations with higher-positioned individuals | Understanding diversity and tailoring your communication to meet those needs | Choosing the correct medium for maximum impact |

Soft skills are not easy to teach and are not always easy for a person to change. It is not like teaching keyboarding. Much of a person's interpersonal skill polish comes from within. I say it is in a person's DNA. Some people are just naturally good at delivering bad news and others are not. Certain individuals maintain a good attitude no matter what is going on at work or home; and other people are not. I don't want you to think this is hopeless as I have taught tens of thousands of administrative professionals how to develop, fine tune, and master their interpersonal and soft skills.

Please do not believe anyone who says, "Soft skills aren't important. It's all about technology today." Employers are more interested in the soft skills because that is hard to change in a person. A person can go to a class on Excel or PowerPoint. Just think about those in your workplace who have a bad attitude or communicate aggressively or speak before they think … how are they perceived by others at your office? I'm sure not in a positive fashion.

## WHAT NOW?

As a result of reading this chapter, what action steps are you going to take in the next 30 days to move in the right direction?

1. _____

_____

2. _____

_____

3. _____

_____


## WHAT OTHER THOUGHTS COME TO MIND?

_____

_____

# CHAPTER
# 28

# BE BUSINESS
# SAVVY

**I DID NOT GO** to college or business school by choice. I went right into the business world and started working as a receptionist. I was immediately fascinated by business. I loved the dynamics of the workplace (even though it was sometimes frustrating). I especially soaked up watching the 'higher-ups' in the office. I was intrigued by how they managed everything and their business smarts.

I wasn't a receptionist for long as I had big dreams of being an executive assistant. Growing up and starting my career in Cleveland, Ohio allowed me to work at a variety of substantial businesses and industries. I had two favorite places. I worked at the Higbee Company in downtown Cleveland. It was a twelve-story department store. You might not remember what a department store is because they don't exist anymore. But it was such an exciting place to work and so much fun! I worked as the executive secretary to the Vice President of Human Resources. Ted was a very nice boss and smart. He brought me into the business by taking time to explain the industry and our company to me. I was a sponge, as usual. It was quite fun interacting with so many different departments and, once again, I observed the higher-ups' actions, behaviors, and speech. I started to select what I liked and what I didn't like and tucked it in my back pocket.

The other place of business I dearly loved was Fabri-Centers of America. They owned Jo-Ann Fabric Shops. Do you remember those? They are now called Joann Fabrics and Crafts. I was an eager executive assistant to one of the top executives. We had 16 district supervisors who reported to my executive. Our corporate office had many moving pieces and departments. The business was vast. I got to sit in the premiere place of the entire company. My work area was positioned in a beautiful all-glass entry. While I was an executive assistant, I also had the privilege of greeting many high-profile visitors who came to do business. Once again, I watched, observed, and soaked in everything I could about people, behavior, and business.

I cannot emphasize enough the importance of you gaining perspective on business. I also know for a fact that at the writing of this book (2018), executives are expecting their assistants to have common knowledge of business—understanding terminology, basic financials, budgeting, forecasting, and industry terminology. You might also look into business and financial cycles. I understand this may be a real challenge for you, but this truly is a secret because many assistants are not even aware they should be learning about business. One caution: reading a business book is different than talking to people who are in the trenches and running businesses, so I would do both.

If you are fortunate enough to have an executive or another leader in your organization who is willing to teach you or provide some explanation of why they do what they do and make the decisions they make, then soak it up! They are worth their weight in gold.

## WHAT NOW?

As a result of reading this chapter, what action steps are you going to take in the next 30 days to move in the right direction?

1. _____
   _____

2. _____
   _____

3. _____
   _____

## WHAT OTHER THOUGHTS COME TO MIND?

_____

_____

# Office Dynamics Workplace Tools

Office Dynamics provides a broad range of solutions for administrative office professionals and their executives. Please check out the following services and products at our website below.

**Annual Conference for Administrative Excellence**

**On- and Off-site Training**

**Keynote and Motivational Speeches**

**Monday Motivators (free weekly enote)**

**World Class Assistant™ Certificate and Designation Program**

**Star Achievement Series® Certificate and Designation Program**

**Webinars**

**Live E-Courses**

**Joan Burge Blog (at OfficeDynamics.com)**

**Executive and Assistant Coaching**

**And Much More!**

For More Information
Visit www.OfficeDynamics.com
Call 800-STAR-139

CPSIA information can be obtained
at www.ICGtesting.com
Printed in the USA
BVHW07s1337240918
528340BV00029B/1256/P